A Treasured Island

Rachel Anne Maxwell

Lockeport, NS

Copyright © 2004 Rachel Anne Maxwell
All rights reserved. Except for the quotation of short passages for review purposes, no part of this publication may be reproduced in any form without prior permission of the author.

Design: Brenda Conroy
Cover: Watercolour of Tancook Island by Hugh Lane-Davies
Back cover photo: Rachel Anne Maxwell, circa 1985, on Tancook Island
Printed and bound in Canada by
Sentinel Printing, Yarmouth, NS

Copies of this book may be obtained from:
Ron Stockton or Bernadette Maxwell
(902) 422-6055, fax (902) 429-7655
(902) 624-0733, fax (902) 624-0242

Published by Community Books
RR1, Lockeport, Nova Scotia, B0T 1L0
phone/fax: (902) 656-2223
email: kathleen.tudor@ns.sympatico.ca
www.selfpublishingspecialists.com

Library and Archives Canada Cataloguing in Publication

Maxwell, Anne, 1919-
A treasured island / Rachel Anne Maxwell.

ISBN 1-896496-46-6

1. Maxwell, Anne, 1919- —Anecdotes. 2. Tancook Island (N.S.)—Anecdotes. I. Title.

FC2345.T35Z49 2004   C818'.603   C2004-905686-7

Contents

Chapter 1	Hearsay	5
Chapter 2	Settlers and Sellers	9
Chapter 3	Neighbour	28
Chapter 4	Haunting	41
Chapter 5	The Making of Gardens	56
Chapter 6	Harry	71
Chapter 7	Happy Fall	80
Chapter 8	Hearing	85
Chapter 9	Roses	87
Chapter 10	Flotsam and Jetsam	93
Chapter 11	Up in the Green Dell, Down on the Liar's Bench	106
Chapter 12	High Summer	132
Chapter 13	Updating a Wedding	150
Chapter 14	Zucchinis and Forestry	173
Chapter 15	The Laws of Which Land	182
Chapter 16	Sea Changes	196

To the Islanders

Chapter 1

Hearsay

*And silence, like a poultice, comes
To heal the blows of sound.*
— Oliver Wendell Holmes, Sr.

They say the house is haunted, as is the road past the old graveyard where a phantom dog snarls periodically. Some of them do, anyhow, those who have seen Jacob's face staring through the tiny window he cut years ago in the east wall of the kitchen so that he could watch the winding hill sixty yards away, see who was coming or going to the bay.

They say a lot of things here. Words run around the Island like quicksilver and as they run, they change their shape. A couple of miles slipping kitchen to kitchen, a few minutes in the store or the post-office and Jimmy's idle question on the wharf: "Why ain't the Mary Lou home yet?" may have swollen into a shipwreck or a who-dun-it.

In our little kitchen, which used to be Jacob's, the word only has to fly a foot or two before it is transformed by the imagination which has become the compensation for M.D.'s failing ears. So we say things like this:

Me: (trying not to be dogmatic about something or other) I'm just fairly sure…

M.D.: (hating his given name, I have always called him "My Darling," even when he was tiresome) *Really?* You saw a *fairy?* or,

Me: (getting ready to catch the ferry) I want to start packing up…

M.D.: (pause) *Really?* You want a little *harp?*

or, when he needed help to fix the recalcitrant woodsplitter on a ferociously cold day, he suggested getting Neighbour's husband, William, down:

Me: "No, you can't bring an old man like William out…"

M.D.: "I can't get an *adult?*"

So then it's:

Me: (with voice raised) "No, perhaps we need a fairy with a little harp — an adult one, preferably."

M.D.: (enlightened at last) "That's it exactly. *Then* the damned thing would work…"

* * *

William, a tall, lanky fellow, carries his years well, and his seaman's eyes still see far and clear without glasses; but I noticed the other day when he was down sampling a glass of the latest home-made wine at our kitchen table that he now wears a hearing-aid in his left ear. What if M.D. got himself one — or even two? I must consult Neighbour and find out whether communication with her man has become more effective or merely less humorous since he agreed to buy the gadget. Who knows whether M.D. would make much more sense of what I actually say if he heard me perfectly the first time? Part of his difficulty will still be that he is deeply absorbed in complicated thoughts — far beyond my ken — about his computer, his wine-making, his boat. Age exaggerates us all: he grows more focussed in his thinking, I am increasingly diffuse and scattered. Perhaps this happy difference would still guarantee an element of surprise and entertainment in our talk, sufficient to keep us from sinking into total banality anyhow.

"Did you hear about the appalling problems with irrigation in Africa on the radio?" I asked him brightly at lunch today.

"Problems with *urination*?" Astonished disbelief. Some new disease, perhaps? Because his background is medical, words will slide into a clinical, rather than an ecological, context as they reach him.

Yes, it may be time to call on modern technology. Some of it is useful, I hear.

* * *

On a calm summer's day, the islands between us and the mainland look like a peaceful flock of green sheep resting in a blue pasture.

Now, under a sky heavy with probable snow, they are small dead dinosaurs dotting the grey watery wilderness — a dozen or more visible from my kitchen window. Beyond them, when the long night falls shortly, lights will twinkle in mainland village houses; but the islands will be invisible. Nobody lives on them.

Here, though, I will look up the hill to make sure Neighbour's window is lit — all must be well with her — and across the little bay to the wharf. The lights there show the ferry is safely berthed; it will chug off again on its voyage to the mainland before dawn. But now that our house is insulated as well as banked with spruce boughs, and the double-windows are sealed against winter gales, I shall not hear it leave, despite my good ears.

We are well into the months of silence — five of them. It is the time of year when, to some extent, I share M.D.'s loss of hearing; we are cut off from all the normal Island sounds. The north kitchen window shows only a silent movie; fish boats appear and disappear with no warning from their motors, flocks of crows rage at each other soundlessly, gulls open their cruelly hooked beaks in fury and I can only guess at what they are screeching at each other; but, worst of all, the wind will shout and whistle, the waves will crash on the rocks, the trees bend and creak in the gale, the spray from the foaming water blow over us — and I shall hear nothing of all the fine commotion.

When we came here nearly twenty years ago, the house was a sieve — all the winds of heaven blew noisily through it, under the pine floors with shrivelled, ineffective oakum between the boards, through the ancient windows with bubbly glass and worn mullions, around the ill-fitting doors. We were cold that first winter, but we knew what was going on beyond our four walls, even on a moonless night. Now we are warm but deaf, both of us, to the outside world; we live in an island of silence in an island alive with a thousand sounds.

Chapter 2

Settlers and Sellers

*Oh, was there ever sailor free to choose
That didn't settle somewhere near the Sea?*
— Kipling

The population is in a free-fall — a third of what it was at the turn of the century, only about three hundred souls. But our ghosts are neither dying off nor seeking an easier life on the mainland. According to the talkative lad, Pat, in the cottage by the road, they are all over the place.

We had only been here a few days when he came to the door.

"I were wondering whether you needs any help? Things to do before the cold comes, say…"

"Not just now, but thanks anyhow."

Everybody wanted to get a closer look at the foreigners, which is what all mainlanders are to any Islander, and all were curious to know what was going on in the old house; but what Pat was chiefly interested in was an answer to his next question:

"Jacob been bothering you yet? I seen him at the little window again when you was away yesterday."

Disappointingly, for Pat, Jacob was paying no attention to us; and we were so fully occupied dealing with the other inhabitants of the house that we would scarcely have had a minute to pass the time of day with him if he had. Armies of wood-lice bivouacked in dark corners, sending out foraging parties hither and yon; cities of carpenter ants left small mounds of marvellously fine sawdust at regular intervals to show that they were still hard at work in corner-post or beam; mice moved their families indoors to take advantage of newly available food; and the variety of spiders peacefully spinning webs was remarkable.

* * *

Jacob had died, in his eighties, four years before our arrival and the house had stood abandoned ever since. After the funeral, the daughters set to and cleaned the whole place from top to bottom, washed and dried the hooked mats, placing all forty of them in a neat pile in the attic and folded up the feather ticks and rough hand-woven blankets. The old crockery remained on the three shelves in the tiny pantry, where Jacob did his dishes in the stone sink under his peep-hole window. There were no water-pipes to be drained, no furnace to be switched off, and neither sons nor daughters took anything away from the fish-store, the barn or the house itself. Once everything was in good order, they simply snibbed the tiny padlock on the door and walked away from it all. The old stuffed owl on the parlour mantel looked down, unblinking, from his perch on clean emptiness.

* * *

While the seven children were young, Jacob provided for the family in the usual Island way by fishing, farming and, most lucrative, rum-running. This last being a risky business, a prudent man might take steps to secure his property in case he was caught by the guardians of law and order; a heavy fine might mean having to sell his land. Jacob, therefore, paid a lawyer in Oldham to draw up a fancy deed, making all that he owned over to his wife. What was not his could not be taken from him, he trusted.

Effie was a good partner for someone in her husband's complex line of work. She always had her wits about her, which was especially necessary when the excise men descended on the Island. Jacob was out at his nets when she pulled one of her neatest tricks, but he must have been pleased with her performance when he reached home.

On a summer's morning, the youngest boy ran into the kitchen screaming: "The men's comin' up the hill!" Effie stopped peeling carrots and shouted for the rest of the children. By the time the excise men began thumping on the door, Effie was in the parlour playing the harmonium, the children gathered round her. She looked up with a smile as they tramped into the room behind the little son who had opened the door to them.

"Do join us for a hymn," she said brightly and when, a trifle abashed, they answered that they had orders to search the house, not sing, she urged them to go ahead.

They never knew that Effie was seated on a fair-sized barrel of rum, her long skirts spread over it, as the family delivered their tuneless version of "Nearer, My God, to Thee." She had had the children roll it into place quickly before the knock on the door.

Effie died suddenly and too young — appendicitis, no medical help. Her will left all her property to the seven offspring, jointly, and nothing to the husband who, in the normal course of things, should have been in the grave long before her.

A guest in his children's home, Jacob watched them

grow, marry and, most of them, move to the mainland. Alone in the end, after the last son, who had lived for some years in bachelor's quarters — a room he had built onto the west wall of the house — had moved away, Jacob set about making himself comfortable in his old age. He closed off the downstairs rooms and the high beamed attic where the children had slept in narrow spool-beds under the bare roof-boards, and confined his life to the kitchen. Here he had the faithful warmth of the fine wood-stove, the view of the bay from his window, his tiny scullery with the peephole to the east, and there was also a cupboard of a room on the opposite side. In this, he placed a fancy modern bed, ordered from the new-fangled Eaton's mail-order catalogue, a *spring* mattress for aging bones. For awhile, he kept up a bit of a vegetable garden on the cliff-top, but in due course, he gave that up and was satisfied when Neighbour took to bringing him her own vegetables and the lad next door began bringing him wood for the stove and a couple of buckets of water from what was their common well in those days.

It was not a bad life for an old man, and company was provided by the school children who trooped over after class. At his kitchen table, Jacob entertained, educated and corrupted them. He had a rich store of tales of rum-running days, vividly embroidered, no doubt, for the benefit of his goggle-eyed audience. There were many ways of hiding the rum after the runners had survived the hazards at sea — for instance, a hidden cave dug out behind a root cellar served well at times. And he could point the finger at certain bad characters who had ratted on their neighbours to the excise men because of some feud or other, over land usually. The day's history lesson over, Jacob went on to instruct the children in more immediate matters such as how

Settlers and Sellers

to play poker and how to smoke; they watched him as he rolled the cigarettes he sold them one at a time. The knife-marks where he cut the tobacco are still visible on the table at which we eat. Pine, being soft, tells more stories than oak or birch.

Once, a couple of decades ago, we were approached by an enterprising fellow from the loop road who wanted to go into partnership with M.D. and get a tavern going; having other fish to fry, we declined. The Island amenities are therefore still limited to one small store, one small school, and two churches. The churches are physically separated by half a mile; theologically by some minute fundamentalist difference and politically by a fair amount of back-biting rivalry; but they are, of course, united in prescribing teetotalism. For the non-devout majority of our population, the liquor now crosses the water quite legally from Oldham; on Friday evenings especially, the freight boxes are laden with sufficient bottles to ensure a cheery weekend. The women Jacob taught to gamble when they were small girls now hold bingo evenings in the community centre. The men play poker elsewhere and a good many of both sexes have renounced the wicked weed lately since modern health propaganda has reached even our shores.

* * *

Looking from her window just up the hill, Neighbour noticed one winter's morning that there was no smoke curling up from Jacob's chimney. It was she who came down and found him dying quietly on the pine floor beside his grand mail-order bed. He had had a stroke and rolled out helplessly when he had tried to get up and feed the stove.

Neighbour was then, and will be as long as she lives, the

one who knows something is wrong, even if there is no smoke signal, and quietly does something about it. She is essential to the Island's well-being; but even she could not find a way through the impasse in which Jacob's children entangled themselves after they had buried him. Some, the less prosperous ones, wanted to sell the property and get their share of the proceeds. Others wanted to keep it as a place to visit in the summer. After three years of bitter argument, most of those who were holding out for continued ownership lost patience and agreed to sell; it was six against one for another year of vituperation before the last daughter capitulated and signed. To avoid further misery, all of the children also now agreed, wearily, to leave the contents of house and out-buildings as they were at the time of Jacob's death. His ghost, therefore, kept all his familiar possessions around him, and we, with fortuitous good timing, were able to buy a fully furnished house, together with barns stuffed with every type of useful implement from axes and saws, hoes and shovels to scallop-rakes, miles of cod-line, coiled up in barrels, and a few ancient lobster-traps. We heard later that the long wrangling over the fate of the house left the family so deeply scarred that two of the sisters refused to talk to their siblings for twenty years. Anyone who has tried it a few times is likely to have learnt that buying or selling a house takes one onto dangerous ground; after all, it is more than a building that is being exchanged. It is also a home, and most of us like to hope there is an old one to come back to or a new one waiting to be created — our own.

We first saw the house and the Island on Bastille Day, 1972. We had noticed, passing through Oldham on a weekend excursion from the city, a dingy little photograph of an old cottage standing, apparently, in a hay-field but looking

Settlers and Sellers

straight out to sea. The price, under the snap in the real estate agent's window was, to a mainlander, astonishingly small. With a little luck, we might even be able to rake up such a sum. Wild surmise. Would it suddenly be possible, after nearly forty years, to live beside the sea again? We phoned the agent, who told us to go over and take a look at the place any time we felt like it. Plainly, not an ardent saleswoman; but then her commission would not amount to much. The neighbour up the hill behind the house had the key and would let us in, she said, and hung up.

The keeper of the key was out in her garden weeding, a small woman, dressed for hard work in old slacks, a faded shirt, a bright kerchief over greying hair. Probably she was trying to size us up as she accompanied us down the grassy slope between her cottage and Jacob's: what sort of foreigners might be about to land up almost on her doorstep? But she asked no idle questions, would wait to find out. "Just snib the padlock when you're through" she said and left us to our own devices while she hurried back to her vegetables. If I had realised then how important suitable neighbours are on a small island, I would have paid more attention to her.

By the time we had explored the little house, so silent that one wondered whether one should whisper within its walls, walked along the cliff top and up a mossy path into the spruce woods, boarded the ferry again, M.D. and I were in silent as well as verbal agreement. Being youngish at that time, he could hear, and often got the gist of my irrational words. On that day, I made them very clear and they tallied exactly with his feelings.

On the upper deck, still warmed by the quietly sinking sun, his hair blowing around in the small breeze, he stood in the stern, gazing contemplatively at the foaming wash. I sat on a bench up in the bow watching a historical mental movie, oblivious to the beauty of this particular summer's evening. The film might have been titled: Joy and Sorrow. The blurb underneath could have read: Plenty of excitement! Worth seeing again! And don't forget the laughs!

One or two of the more dramatic episodes caught my fancy and I slowed the reel down in order to see the details more clearly.

There was, for instance, an early 1950s one — ancient history in these hurtling times, but still well-preserved. We were out on the West Coast, happily impecunious because M.D. was still not quite through the interminable postgraduate work which had naturally been interrupted by the war: from 1943 until Christmas 1945, he had been binding up the wounds of a Canadian regiment in Normandy, Belgium and Holland, as well as those of civilians along the way. Now the government was nobly repaying him by giving him $204.06 monthly while he studied to specialise. He had no complaints; the powers that be had already granted him a severance gratuity of $2,000, which we used as a down payment to put a roof over our heads. The groceries never cost more than $15 a week, the mortgage was $50 monthly and, of course, there was no car to finance. We got plenty of exercise, M.D. walking to the hospital, me pushing a baby buggy hither and yon; no need to pay a spa or gym to keep us healthy. Entertainment was free too — from the public library; shelling out money to go to a show was a very rare event. The idea of having a column in the family budget marked "Entertainment" would have struck us as ridiculous anyhow. On different sides of the western world, we had both grown up making our own amusements and for the last several years, we had been fully occupied merely surviving — "boredom" was a word we scarcely knew. Merely being alive after the cataclysm sufficed; only at night, when the three children were finally asleep, was there time to wonder yet again what finger of fate had allowed us to live when millions didn't. My mind would be crowded with young memories of dead brothers, cousins, friends, glimpses of the inside of a concentration camp M.D. had seen in 1945, until grateful sleep came at last.

As soon as mail resumed between Britain and France after the long silence of the war, I sent a note to a Jewish friend from student days in Paris — 1938, 1939. I was to have been a bridesmaid that summer in her grand synagogue wedding... There was scant hope she would get my news of the deaths, the births in my extended family over the last six years, but she did and replied immediately. "What a holocaust," she said, referring to my brothers and cousins, a number of whom she had known; her family and mine mingled regularly before the war. The word had not then taken on its final meaning and, of course, her "holocaust" had been far more dreadful than mine or those of my mother, my aunts — lovers and brothers lost in one war, sons in the next. I bear the name of an uncle killed at Gallipoli, two of my sons bear those of my brothers, one buried in Hong Kong, the other dead from his experience of hell in the jungles of Burma, a third that of an almost-brother cousin, torpedoed in a troopship only some thirty miles east of where I sat that afternoon on the deck watching the past flicker by. Sara was driven to give her wartime child an unmistakably Christian name, even had him baptized to add to his chances of survival. In an unjust world, M.D. and I had been enabled to escape recent history, embark on making successive homes from the west coast to the east of this wide New World, sell one and buy a replacement again and again. If we achieved the purchase of the Island house, it would be our seventh haven. A lucky number, perhaps the apotheosis would come to pass? And on my birthday, too? It would be better than any of the wild celebrations I once shared with France.

But first, with the help of the old film, consider possible obstacles to the consummation of the deal, methods of overcoming them should they arise. Attentive again to the images from the early 1950s, I watched the older children dutifully trudging off to school from the back porch, homework carefully completed in leather satchels on their narrow backs, M.D. rushing off to the hospital through the front door. He was always rushing then and for decades after: too many solutions to too many scientific problems and not enough time to encompass them all. The youngest child was playing with the devoted Alsatian in the back yard, in the shadow of the great chestnut tree decked for a new spring with a thousand candles of blossom. Time to drink my coffee, cold by then, collect myself, and carry on. Nine heavy months pregnant, I collapsed at the kitchen table and called a real estate agent.

The house was pleasant, I told him — in good shape, four bedrooms, a magnificent chestnut in the back yard, a graceful acacia in the front one (the trees did not seem to interest him much), not too old (wooden houses die young in those parts), and it must be sold at once. The urgency in my voice galvanised him into immediate action; he came round and ran through the place that afternoon. Soon after noon the next day, a van drew up on our street, a tall fellow with a beard got out and walked around the house, which stood on a good corner lot — a plus, a selling point, I thought to myself, watching him from a window, with or without trees. His exterior survey completed, he rang the bell. Might he see the inside of the place? Hope of a rapid sale welling up, quite irrationally, I took him over it, enthusiastically pointing out the beauty of the polished oak floors (we could not afford the then fashionable carpets so I carried on laboriously waxing them monthly) and the amenities, which included a new-fangled Bendix washing-machine. I did not tell him that often my friends would bring their laundry over and share a cup of tea with me sitting on the floor in front of it while it did its amazing work, visibly, through a round window. We were mesmerised by its behaviour, as later generations have been by T.V. and other gadgets; probably it did us less harm. And I did not enjoy the thought of leaving it for the pleasure of new owners of the house. Nevertheless, we must sell, and immediately. The child within me was getting restive but I could not take time off to give birth to it; it was essential for me to stick around, dust, sweep, be pleasant to would-be buyers until a sale went through. We had committed a folly, signed a legal document to buy another property two weeks previously, without the resources to do it. The bank would not help us; they had meanly bounced a small cheque carelessly written the other day, although they knew that the government came through with something regularly. All we owned was the present house, or at least a bit of it.

The face of that first prospective buyer was fuzzy on the old film, except for the bushy beard. It and its owner sat opposite me in our pleasant living room after his tour of the house and the audio part of the film was clear as he said "I like it. Suits me fine. Now let's get down to brass tacks."

He gestured towards the tall windows. "See that van out there? It's piled high with beaver pelts — I just came down from the North. How would that do for a down-payment? They're going up in value every day, you know." I didn't, but went out with him to admire their glossy beauty. We didn't have time to get into the fur market; reluctantly, I sent him over to friends nearby who were also selling a house and might have the freedom to look into pelts. The wife was not pregnant, nor were they broke.

A couple of days later, an old lady turned up on the doorstep, brought by a taxi. The front door bell. Hooray! Another prospect, bound to be more reasonable than the first, surely. She was gasping for breath after climbing the porch steps as I welcomed her in. Dear Lord, was she going to have a heart attack on the spot, before she could even make an offer? I settled her on the living room couch and left her to recover quietly while I put on a kettle. Maybe a cup of tea would help? Or should I try a spoonful of brandy, the universal Victorian remedy? Neither was needed; when I returned to the living room, her pleasantly wrinkled cheeks were a good colour, her old eyes bright and she was anxious to begin the tour of inspection. An expensive well-cut coat, I noticed, as I led her round the ground floor, white hair elegantly coiffed, a whiff of lavender as she moved: she should have the where-with-all for a good down-payment. She appeared to find the sunny high-ceilinged rooms attractive; but she balked at the sight of the stairs.

"Quite enough down here for me," she said happily. "Everything I need!" It was true that there was a toilet in the small Bendix room, but was the absence of a bath of no concern to her? "Let's talk business — I want to make you an offer right away, I'd be cross if somebody else got in first and you never know who might come along."

Trying to "talk business" was uphill work: the total price of the property, taxes, mortgage arrangements and so on were of no more interest to her than the location of the bath. Perhaps she was simply certain that far more than enough cash was waiting for her just around the corner — or rather at the finishing post a few miles away? For the down-payment with which she was trying very hard to tempt me was a half-share in the winnings of a horse she owned, due to run in an important race in three or four weeks time. As she rattled on almost lyrically about the splendid talents of the animal, its pretty gaits, the excellence of the jockey, the inevitability of the coming triumph, the size of the purse she would share with us in exchange for the house, I became charmed, intrigued by her love for her horse; but not quite seduced by her offer.

"I'll talk it over with my husband," I assured her, showing her out. The obedient taxi-driver was waiting. Somehow she looked a little less soigné than when she had arrived, although the sweet scent of Yardley's Olde English Lavender, after her display of enthusiasm, was a little stronger. Before I could let her know the result of the consultation with my spouse, a son of the old gambling addict phoned to say she was not actually in the market for a fair-sized house, although she did have a habit of trying to collect them, as well as race-horses. A kindly son.

The background of the old film shifted from the pleasant family house in old Vancouver to more interesting places beyond the city and I had to admit that we too were gamblers, devious ones at that. And we did not have the excuse of adventurous senility. Some months previously, carless, cashless, we had hit on the idea of taking an occasional Sunday afternoon jaunt for free with someone who had a vehicle — and gas to run it — fun for the kids, anyhow, amusing for us. By chance, we hit on an expatriate European real estate agent who got in the habit of picking us all up now and again and ferrying us hither and yon. I don't think we actually told her the truth, namely that we were not really planning to move: there are duplicitous buyers as well as sellers. Maybe she just guessed things about us that we did not know ourselves or had not thought about and sensed that we might be induced to buy. In any case, one Sunday afternoon, she turned the tables on us.

Vignettes appeared on the screen of several unusual houses she had shown us, one an almost circular building on the West Vancouver mountainside, said to have been designed decades ago by a royal prince as a love-nest for his mistress. (Which prince? Which mistress? The film did not say.) It had been a fascinating outing but the children were growing weary. Time to be driven home but, "On the way, we'll just drop in for a moment at a *really* special place. It's worth a look, I promise you." One cannot argue with the chauffeur, especially if she has become a friend. The property certainly did not lie on the quick route to the city over one or other of the bridges — Lion's Gate, Burrard. Instead, the little car into which we were squashed began to climb the precipitous, narrow road straight up the face of the North Vancouver mountains. It was known as a "Highway" then but, unless it has grown much wider in the last number of years, it would not rate so noble a name today. Almost at the tree-line, we veered off to the right along an even narrower road. Above us rose the dark forest, secret in its density, close but still inviolable. We had heard that a rash woman had ventured into its depths recently and never been seen again; the entangling undergrowth of those old trees had imprisoned her, was the supposition. Only a few hundred yards off the "Mountain Highway," past a couple of dilapidated frame cottages, we came upon the "really special place."

Our agent had been telling the truth. Through enormous double gates, we swept around the curving, well-paved driveway and parked under a porte-cochère wide enough to shelter a carriage and four or a Rolls Royce. Below us stretched a long and well kept garden of lawns and flower beds, just visible at its foot a tiny cottage behind an apple tree. Before us stood, incongruously, a half-timbered Tudor mansion. What on earth was it doing in these still pioneer surroundings? Fatigue forgotten, we willingly went in to explore. The children, suddenly rejuvenated, ran up and down the broad oak staircases, shouting to each other from storey to storey — there were three of them — "Come and look at this." Two vast living rooms lay empty of life but pleasantly furnished one above the other, both giving onto the garden through French doors; I did not shout, but a happy thought crossed my mind: "Could we consign the kids to their own splendid nether regions, attend peacefully to our own concerns well above them?" Five bedrooms on two levels, two nameless small rooms, a magnificent workshop in the high basement, which plainly appealed greatly to M.D., a conservatory off it, a wide verandah running round the south and east walls, a mountain stream rushing down beside the house to pause briefly in a pool under tall trees…

"Who on earth would want to sell such a paradise?" we asked the canny agent who was watching us with a half-smile on her sensible face. She explained that the gardening wife of the wealthy owner had developed arthritis, could now only cope with a rock-garden. They had bought a magnificent, self-sufficient one, with house attached, in suburban West Vancouver and were eager to move. This property was hard to sell because of its very unfashionable and inaccessible location; hence, the ridiculously low price, less than that of a modern bungalow in the city. It was isolated here in the sticks because of its romantically unlikely genesis, which began in the First World War when a Canadian soldier wooed and won an aristocratic but adventurous English girl. He would bring her back to his western ranch, he swore, and she would love it. Unfortunately, the ranch turned out to be the clapboard cottage, now at the bottom of the garden, with a few acres of wilderness around it, the primeval forest looming above it. The husband soon drank himself to death and the young woman took in washing to feed her two children until one day she learnt that she had inherited a quarter of a million dollars — real money, in those days — from an aunt. I could not easily read the name of this benefactress on the old film but I believe it was Lady Horner, who had wisely married a "merchant prince" of the late Victorian establishment — boat-building money, I rather think; in any case, considerable. She was childless, however, so the North Vancouver niece shared the estate with her sister in England. Immediately, she hired the best architect available, a Mr. Blackadder, who designed and built her dream-home with extraordinary skill. The cottage was tactfully moved down the property far from the new mansion — was it preserved as a memorial to a gift from the gods or as a useful lodging for "estate help"? A year or two after the fortunate widow and her children moved into their palatial "English" home, her sister died unexpectedly, leaving her

Settlers and Sellers

another quarter of a million. It was then that the garden was born, a famous landscape artist hired to lay out the unusual terrain, exotic plants and trees brought in from distant places, including some from the Prince of Wales' Alberta ranch. When the widow herself died just as the Second World War broke out, her heirs, busy with their own young concerns, sold the place for a song to the present owner, who did not meddle with its initial perfection but maintained everything in excellent order.

Could it be possible that the fruits of old Lady Horner's munificence might descend, in 1953, to us? A mad dream, from a practical point of view. What about the accessibility of schools for the children, money for upkeep, transportation to work? Details, to be dealt with later, M.D. and I, in our suddenly adopted role as gamblers (as lunatic as the panting old lady I was soon to meet) were thinking as we were driven home over the Burrard bridge. The agent was cheerful — she knew we were hooked, would buy one way or another. A due reward for all those Sunday excursions she had granted us, although it would not be a huge commission, given the picayune price of a key to this particular Eden.

Due to the generosity of one of M.D.'s old professors, who loaned us the down-payment on the mountain home pending the sale of the city place ("Do the same for some other young fools," he said, handing us a cheque, "when I am dead...") and to the good sense of the solid young couple who finally turned up and bought the city house, the new child finally had time to push his way into the world. As soon as that sensible couple signed their offer — $13,000 as I recall, and much more than we had paid for it — I stopped dusting and tidying, had supper, and went to the hospital. The very large boy, overcooked, emerged at midnight, screamed as he should. "Don't call my husband," I told the nurses. "Wait until breakfast time — he's very tired." I was too but, house sold, child born, I fell asleep, happily oblivious of the horrors of my surroundings, the discomfort of the bed, and was ready to greet the father in the morning. We had been through much more inconvenient births in Europe during the war, threatened by bombs and other man-made miseries, and the new child could begin his life on that magnificent mountain-side.

Nevertheless, I have wondered over the years, thinking back to harder times, what it is that drives women to persevere in reproducing the race. Mere biology — replace the dead we have ourselves killed? As far as simpletons like ourselves were concerned, we just enjoyed children, each one unique, unpredictably entertaining, even if we were actually being driven by subterranean forces. And we had no television, CDs, videos and so on in those days to replace the amusement they provided.

Back on the ferry, the film was flickering to the end of the first reel as the Oldham Harbour came into view — just time for a glimpse of the unfortunate middle-aged woman who had so longed to buy that mountain home from us when we were obliged to sell and head east six years later. It was her odd dream, too, as it had been ours. Was she seeing as, apparently entranced, she gazed through the tall living room windows at the garden, the stream, the trees, some lost childhood in another land reincarnated? She had certainly reached the age when one looks back as much as forward. Very different people can share dreams, I was thinking, and not in Freud's sense, as I took her around the house and land. Her taciturn husband brooded gloomily on the sofa meanwhile, refusing to accompany her and when, the tour completed, she said "We'll buy it. I'll call my lawyer in the morning to draw up the offer," he merely stared at her stonily. The couple drove off and three days later the lawyer politely telephoned to tell us there would be no offer; she had now been hired to institute divorce proceedings. Thank God, I thought, as the film ended and the old boat docked at the Oldham wharf, that M.D. and I are still dreaming a similar dream, of woods and water.

The following morning we put in our small offer to the surprised agent. She was glad to remove the dingy snap of the place from her office window (after all, who wants to live on that *Island*?) and the seven owners were probably happy to have the bone of contention removed at last. Buying and selling — what a game it is these days and how different from the times when people were stuck on one small patch of ground, rooted there whatever the difficulties.

Chapter 3

Neighbour

Heart bids mind wonder,
Mind bids heart ponder
—W. de la Mare

February snow fell for nearly two days, blowing and eddying horizontally for one, and then, when the wind dropped suddenly, sifting down small and straight. Through my south kitchen window, I could see the young spruces up the hill standing like a *corps de ballet* in immaculate tutus, their lower branches gleaming with it. Over everything there was a sheen which almost hurt the eyes; when the snow ceased yesterday the sun shone briefly, just enough warmth in it now to smooth the surface, leaving us in a sea of opaque crystalline glass after the hard night frost. But the stove needed logs; I must sully its brittle purity with my boots, tramp out to the woodshed.

When I opened the door I caught my breath. Unmistakable pug-marks led down from the woods, across the half-moon rose-garden, right up to the doorstep. The silly thought rushed through me: "He *is* here on the Island. There is no escape — tigers can swim." For decades, he has haunted my dreams, the Bengal man-eater, and last night he was at it again, padding round the house at his leisure, waiting for that perfect moment in which to snatch a child, or, now, a

Neighbour

grandchild, and drag it off into the jungle. I knew his sovereign cunning from long ago and on other continents, and to what ends he had developed it; I had become ever more knowledgeable in the forests of my nights.

Tigers, they used to say in Bengal a hundred years ago, are not by nature man-eaters; they get the habit when they are driven to it by some injury which impairs their normal hunting prowess. My tiger is slightly lame in his right front leg; for several years he used to moan softly as he paced through the sleeping house.

The children, or grandchildren, always find him exotically charming, the most entrancing of all the pets we've ever owned, from snakes and goats and rabbits to a homeless pony or two, a couple of stray Alsatians, and, once, a terrifying tiny shrew. Each time he leaps into my quiet sleep, his yellow eyes gleam with a half-smile behind them; he knows that I am alone in divining his brutal scheme — and totally powerless to foil it. What can one woman do, after all, in the face of a wall of incomprehension?

"Stop fussing," says M.D. sensibly. In my dreams, he is no longer deaf to my words, only to their meaning. "He's a splendid playmate for the kids, gentle as a kitten…" and he sets off down to the shore to paint the boat. Meanwhile, the tiger has been up in the attic for ten minutes, padding softly round the rooms, sniffing at scattered toys, his unblinking eyes on the children as they play. Now and then, one or other of them comes over to him, pats his broad head, runs a small hand over his glistening striped flank. Suddenly he bounds down the staircase; the children, chattering excitedly, follow him into the parlour. They don't seem to notice the animal's fetid odour; and he has not yet bared his teeth to them, nor unsheathed his claws.

So, to avoid the final horror, I wake, go to the kitchen, shake the ashes and, warmed by the stove, read a book which has nothing to do with India. The sinuous lovely creature is banished; but only until another night in which he wishes to roam.

It was, I realised as soon as I had slammed the door shut, the delicate paw prints of Neighbour's feral cat which had marked the pristine snow yesterday. The transient warmth of the afternoon sun had swollen them to fit a full-grown tiger before the starry night fell.

A great many things I share with Neighbour, who is only two or three years younger than me — but not the tiger; I shall not tell her what a fright her cat gave me. The women here have their own night visitors, and they are more likely to come from the sea than the jungle. Up in the graveyard several old stones carry one word cut below the name: "Drowned." Sometimes when I sit by the stove in the small hours, I see a light go on suddenly round the bay at Beatrice's house. I am not the only old woman awake.

Neighbour has only lived off the Island for a year or two, just long enough to know that there is no better place to be on this strange planet. My life, begun in India, trailing across Europe and from the Pacific to the Atlantic in Canada, might make our friendship unlikely except that this small island and the ocean all around it mean the same to her, the native, as they do to me, the immigrant.

From her kitchen window, looking down the hill over our cottage to the bay, she watched our arrival and settling in. Through the years, she had seen several other foreigners move into some old house or other, seeking a sea-girt utopia which would cure them of all the ills of modern civilisation. She knows, and I know, that there is no cure, even here. We bring it with us, our original sin. It was rooted here long before our arrival and was never especially original, anyhow; those who live surrounded by the ocean must come to terms with the rhythm of its tides, its blind furies as well as its evening peace when a path of rippled gold joins the shore to the sinking sun, and with the vagaries of the human species.

So Neighbour waited to see what we, the latest strangers on the Island, would make of things here, observing us from up the hill with the same tender acuity she brings to bear on plants and birds. She knew what we were contending with inside the cottage — no running water, small heat, a leaking roof, crumbling horsehair plaster on the old walls — and, of course, outside it.

A spring noon came when I climbed the hill to fetch the mail from the post-office across the road from her house.

"Good morning, Neighbour," she called from her garden. She was hoeing there with quick, skilled movements, a compact little woman with a cotton kerchief on her head and an old jacket on her back against the breeze. "How are your vegetables doing?"

I think she knew already; it was probably she who had encouraged Daniel to come over that first March with his plough to till up Jacob's vegetable patch, long since given over to its own devices. Daniel knew where it lay hidden under the sod on the cliff-top, and revealed it to us after an hour's work — fertile soil, fed with lobster shells, fish heads and seaweed, waiting for seeds. Most of the stones had been removed by the hands of children a hundred years ago; later, we discovered cairns of them in odd places where the buckets were dumped. And she had certainly seen Pat's old mum bring a basket of her seed potatoes down to the resurrected garden and show me how to plant them.

"Seem to be doing fine," I called back to her. "A few shoots up already. Come down and take a look when you have a moment."

* * *

Over the years, we have had many moments. In her kitchen she keeps an old rocking-chair which waits with open arms for visitors. I sit and rock in it, looking out to the bay, when I need advice on such things as keeping cauliflower healthy (pour a bucket of sea-water over the young heads), the best time to plant beans (June 4th, if the moon is right), or how to clean the old stove-stop (a duck's wing was best in time's past; now it's fine sandpaper and wax). Since many other Islanders also rock in that chair (in fact, a spare rocker stands in the corner to accommodate extra visitors), Neighbour can also fill me in with what "they say" in any given week.

She carries on with her cooking or sewing while she talks; her big dining-room table is always spread with bits and pieces of brightly patterned cloth for dressing the dolls she makes when she isn't hooking mats.

Most of the Island women make themselves a small private income with their clever hands and imagination, and Neighbour is famous far and wide for her work. During the great International Exposition of 1967 in Montreal she was recruited to go up and demonstrate her arts to the crowds of tourists from all over the world. They watched her with admiration, then moved on to see William busy at his art, building a wooden boat from scratch, not far away. Deserved glory on the world stage for our little island for a week or two. Neighbour's dolls, whose charming heads are made of apples, have travelled everywhere from Whitehorse to Japan; and an American commissioned her to hook him a twelve by nine foot carpet: that winter she hooked steadily for three months on the huge frame William built her. She produced a masterpiece in an age-old pattern of muted colours, an heirloom for the American, pocket-money and a sense of accomplishment for Neighbour.

So, which of the fearless youths was it who rammed his truck through Sally's fence on Saturday night? (The boys all know, but they're not telling — and Sally's in a rage.) And what about the new boat? Is it to be a car-ferry? (No, thank God! The first petition was rushed through before anybody had time to think, and there was a big fuss; so they had to have another one, and then the women won. The men all wanted to load their catch straight onto their trucks, run them aboard, and deliver the fish right to the fish-plant at Bridport. But how would the women get to Oldham to go to the bank, the doctor, the stores? That's where the wharf was built fifty years ago to serve the first small ferry and that's where she should still dock. Besides, lawless hordes of mainlanders might take advantage of a car-ferry and invade us — imagine what the road would be like with all those extra cars and even motor-bikes!)

The new ferry is merely an updated version of the old one. She can normally take on just one vehicle at a time, and only when the tide is high enough to drive it onto the deck at Oldham and off an hour later at the Island wharf. The right tide rather seldom tallies with her sailing schedule; the operation requires patience and planning.

When there is no urgent news, Neighbour will sometimes take me back through the years to what was being said — and done — decades ago. She can often be more certain of the truth of those old things than of what goes on today; time has sifted and illuminated them.

* * *

"Where were you?" asks M.D. when I return to the house to put on the soup for lunch. This is the coda of my days since his hearing began to fail; I have become for him a silent being, boiling kettles that do not sing, chopping vegetables with a soundless knife, appearing suddenly in a doorway with no warning from my step. When he needs me, there is an anxious edge to his voice: "Where's she gone? Where are you?" as he goes looking. Sometimes I think that will be the last question I shall hear on my death-bed; and then I will not be able to answer.

"Up at Neighbour's," I reply.

"Gossiping again?"

"Of course," I agree. I'm learning the history of the Island: what else is history but the tales we tell each other? And, fortunately for me, my seriously unfashionable view of the subject is a shared one here.

* * *

Our bay is packed with ice this early week in 1992; it is thicker than it has been for fifteen years. At that time, we still had the little old ferry and we watched her butting her way through it like a goat, determined to make her run. Two or three times she was forced to back up and make a second attack at an obstinate floe, but she persevered, reached the thin ice further out with relief and finally a mile or so of open water before entering Oldham harbour. She docked only about forty-five minutes late, battered but still prepared to make the run home.

That little wooden boat creaked and rolled and groaned but never failed us. The only time she abdicated for a few hours was the September day that the great hurricane struck. The crew rushed down to board her as the wind began to roar and the waves grew monstrous. They steered her painfully to open water; she stood out there a mile from land, tumbled around by the tormented sea while the billows thundered over the wharf with such power that they smashed the wooden freight building into kindling, lifted the oil barrels waiting to be delivered and flung them half-way up the grassy hill across the bay as if they were marbles. When it was all over and the little boat dared to limp home, the wharf was unrecognisable, swept clean of everything.

The freight shed has never been rebuilt, so now we must wait without shelter from rain, snow or biting winds to go aboard our grand new ferry. She is built of steel, and as she ploughs calmly out she merely makes strange scratching sounds — giant fingernails scraping her hull — as the ice shatters and parts.

**

"As the days will lengthen, the cold will strengthen," says Neighbour every year in January; but she also says, a little later, "My heart leaped up when I came downstairs this morning and there was the sun peeping in the east window for the first time!" Its arc is wide enough now to cheer us through the remaining weeks of winter.

It was during that last great February freeze-up in the 1970s that Neighbour phoned me one morning. We had watched the transformation of the bay a week earlier. It rarely happens at this end of the century, although in earlier days it was cause for worry if the ice did not grow thick enough to bear men, sleds and animals, and the midwife could not reach the Island for months. One winter Isaac and Joanne, too impatient to wait for spring, walked across the frozen miles to find a minister to marry them; they came home man and wife and remained so for sixty years. This winter again, the waves one day appeared worried, lethargic as the ice began to form; it was as if the palm of a giant hand were pressing down on them. One night they gave up their futile struggle; in the morning there was ice instead of surf, silence instead of ripples on the beach.

"Get on your boots," she said. "There's men up on your headland — I saw them going, with guns. I'll be down in a moment — we'll go up together." There was urgency in her voice.

We found the three men on the cliff-top, preparing to shoot. Their target was a small flock of Canada Geese clustered on the sea-ice; that year, for some reason, they had failed to fly south and were wintering over on the peninsula near Bridport.

Neighbour, usually so mild-voiced, gave the brawny men such a tongue-lashing that they scarcely tried to remonstrate with her.

"What do you think you're doing, shooting those helpless birds?" she wanted to know. "Walking up on this land as bold as brass... No one's got the right to shoot those lovely birds; and don't go pretending you didn't know it's against the law, anyhow. It's a cruel shame you'd even think of it."

Abashed, the men retreated, muttering.

Neighbour and I walked back slowly through the diamond-bright snow, our breath puffing into small clouds in front of our faces.

Through my kitchen window, as we sat over a cup of

coffee, we watched the geese lift from the ice and wheel away towards the peninsula, the sun on their wings.

"They'll live to see another day," said Neighbour, content. Then, irritation back in her voice, "Those men, they'll never grow up. Just because their boats are tied up for now, they have to get their toys out. And they've no need to shoot for food these days."

They have not brought the toys to these acres again; and William soon put up a large sign on his bit of land above us: "No Shooting." It stood there until younger, more irate hunters tore it down one night. They wanted to kill the deer who had swum across from the peninsula and now live shyly in our woods. William was not a fisherman; a ferry captain and boat-builder, he owned no guns.

* * *

My younger brother and I shared a governess for a couple of years in rural England before we were sent off to school, quite well educated by modern standards for our years; I suppose we were seven and eight when she departed for another ill-paid job in the mid-nineteen-twenties. Miss Solomon belonged to the small army of impoverished middle-class Victorian and Edwardian spinsters who adventurously, and untrained of course, went off to Russia to teach the children of aristocrats before the first world war. Bill and I, no aristocrats, received our remarkably concentrated basic instruction for three hours each morning at the same huge table in the day-nursery at which we ate, and, on rainy days, entertained ourselves by building Meccano models, playing Snakes & Ladders or Snap; we were happily self-sufficient and never bored. Our older siblings had somehow intimated to us that we two were "afterthoughts," late and surprising addenda to the peculiar extended family into which they were already half-integrated. They lived beyond the confines of our governessed nursery universe, in remote areas of the rambling old house, and were frequently visited for varying periods, by an assortment of half-orphaned cousins their age, one or other of whose parents had died from cholera (India), "fever" (China), or the 1919 flu pandemic (Australia), as well as a gallery of eccentric aunts and uncles, not all related by blood, often merely by adoption due to long friendship with our parents. This interesting life of the greater household scarcely concerned Bill and me; we lived in our own private one, a great part of it hidden from all other human eyes in the long sloping garden to which we escaped, whenever the weather was remotely agreeable, immediately after our vilely wholesome mid-day meal. The upper half, visible from our nursery windows, was given over to well-kept lawns and flower-beds, but beyond a screen of tall evergreens lay another world: the extensive vegetable and berry garden which fed our whole clan, the unkempt orchard where the goat was tethered, the abandoned stables where we kept our rabbits and guinea pigs (our sister's chickens and ducks lived elsewhere, nearer the old house), and, at the very foot of the slope, a small wilderness guarded by a clump of towering chestnuts. Here, on our own, we continued our education in much the same way that the Island children always did; we learnt how things grow, gathered hints about a sense of responsibility as we cared for our animals, got an inkling about what is now fashionably known as "composting," became familiar with some of the local birds and butterflies. An ordinary struggling middle-class 1920s English rural childhood, but infinitely richer in everything but money than that of the unfortunate modern urban youngster.

Miss Solomon was a tall and awkward woman with straight bobbed black hair, and her heavy horn-rimmed spectacles were forever slipping down her long nose. One day (was it as a reward for having completed our "lessons" in a particularly satisfactory way?) she began to tell us about her past life. Her adventures left us breathless with excitement, and thereafter, until the day she left us, we badgered her for further details. It seemed that during the October Revolution, dreadful things had happened to the noble family she was working for; but somehow she herself had cleverly contrived to escape from the Bolsheviks, all alone. (By now her spectacles were on the very tip of her nose, and Bill and I were on tenterhooks; it was as good as "Robinson Crusoe.") This unlikely heroine had journeyed across acres of steppe, through miles of dark wolf-infested forest, before reaching safety over the Channel in England. I gathered that during the whole length of this epic, perilous journey she had carried under one arm her most precious possession, a Singer sewing machine. An improbable tale perhaps, but one that opened my child's mind to the wonders of history, and even the oddities of geography, as she brought out the dog-eared schoolroom atlas and traced with her bony forefinger, across the pages labelled "Europe," her route home to the Island we lived on.

I look back gratefully to that interim early teacher; she was probably as naturally gifted, in her own odd way, as that other English governess, of whom I heard much later, who taught the Nabokov children sometime around the turn of the century. That woman exhorted her charges, one of them, Vladimir, wrote decades later, to ask themselves three questions before they opened their small mouths to speak:

"Is what I am about to say true? Is it kind? Is it necessary?"

Neighbour had no governess, learnt in other ways; but I have often thought that similar questions are somewhere hidden in her Island mind as she talks. Of course, the asking of them does not dispose of all the problems; leaving aside the difficulties of discovering the truth, even the home truth, to whom one must be kind? On that shining February morning it was the geese and not the hunters Neighbour chose. And it was necessary.

Chapter 4

Haunting

"Curiouser and curiouser," said Alice.
— Lewis Carroll

It was only after several years of peaceful co-habitation with us that Jacob took umbrage at our behaviour; we were quite unprepared for his sudden activity and appalled at its repercussions. At the time, we were merely long weekend, although year-round, Islanders, being a bit too young and too poor to retire properly. It seemed, therefore, only reasonable to invite a lonely lad, seeking a roof over his head for a few months, to use the house in our absences. He was finishing his last year of high school in Oldham and would take the bus in to the city to rejoin his family for the weekends. Jerry was in this predicament because his father, the minister on the Island for the previous year or two, had felt obliged to leave rather suddenly. Here the congregation hires the Reverend, after vetting likely candidates and listening to each one preach a trial sermon. A miniature Day of Judgement, run by the laity. But the one who is hired can also be fired if he does not measure up to expectations; there is a considerable turnover of tenants in the parsonage. One incumbent got into trouble because he used to jog, mainland fashion, up and down the Island every morning for his health. "He'd do better splitting wood for one or other of the old widows," someone said, and others soon agreed. And latterly we had a charming lady minister who preached and sang beautifully with the talented deacon — uplifting duets. But she was slightly suspect from the beginning, in some eyes, because she wore slacks sometimes, high heels often, and even lipstick. Kind and helpful as she was, a middle-aged widow with her own private difficulties, no doubt, she also has gone to the mainland.

Jerry's father displeased, although he was a stirring preacher, because he told too much about his improper early life. How *securely* had he been saved, people began to wonder. And then one Sabbath he charitably, but unwisely, helped William launch his sleek new boat, the Mary Ellen. Was this a fitting thing to do on the Lord's Day? some asked. We, lost souls anyhow, naturally did what we could to aid the laborious operation, bring her out of the boat-shop, take her gently down the steep hill with ropes and pulleys to the waiting water, her make-and-break engine ready to take her anywhere. M.D., with minimal instruction from her designer, had carved her stem with an adze months earlier: he had a stake in her. She was immediately at home on a perfect tide when the ropes came off, a hymn in herself to some Almighty or other, if less graceful, in my eyes, than some of the sailing-boats William used to build.

Our new lodger seemed to be a sensible lad and serious about his work. He had set his sights on becoming a graphic artist, an ambition which turned out to be fortunate, wasn't planning on fooling around after school; in fact, would be too busy with homework to have anybody at all come visiting of an evening. The small upstairs bedroom suited him fine. He could cope with the wood-stove and use a splitting axe, he told us; moreover, short-haired and wearing clean jeans, he looked as if he might keep the place half decent. The father blessed the whole arrangement, even though we were not members of his flock and all seemed well as we sailed off for the mainland on the Monday evening appointed for Jerry's move into the house. And it was neither rowdy school-mates nor our own lack of the right religious attitude which caused the trouble.

* * *

On Friday afternoon, gratefully back on the ferry home, we sensed a curious chill in the air. The Islanders, returning from a couple of hours' shopping, failed to greet us with their normal interested warmth, none of the usual "Down home again, eh?" or "Was it storming in the city on Wednesday too?" People just looked up as we came into the cabin, then carried on with their own conversations. It was an odd sensation. We had waited several years before being unconditionally accepted as part of the fabric of the Island; what on earth had we done suddenly to make us foreigners again? As we chugged across the water in an atmosphere heavy with unspoken suspicion, I pretended to read but my mind was going to an earlier winter. M.D. had decided we needed a new dog to replace a civilised but foolish little animal belonging to a son; it had been run over on a city street. The magnificent Dalmatian was intended to cheer up the mourning boy but the psychology was inept. Anthony agreed politely that it was a fine beast but paid no further attention to it and went on mourning. M.D. was therefore the dog's new owner and we had to bring it with us every weekend. It was an enormously strong creature, all coiled muscle under the elegant spotted coat and devoid of all manners and even of interest in human beings. M.D. took advice and bought a "choke-chain." A true Voltairean Enlightenment man, he has always believed that every dog is trainable just as every man (and *possibly* woman?) is potentially reasonable. The "choking" gadget was intended to control the animal during a gradual breaking-in period; we were to treat it more or less like a newly captured wild horse. The only effect I noticed was a sinister gurgling noise in its throat as it panted up the road from the wharf to the house, dragging me over the ice behind it. Once indoors and off the chain, it leapt onto the couch, stretched out comfortably and bit M.D.'s hand when he tried to turf it off so that we ourselves could relax.

On the ferry, not surprisingly, the Islanders retreated from us as we came aboard with the monster; it had a habit of lurching at anyone within reach, huge teeth alarmingly bared. Sensible people ceased visiting us, knowing what a fiend we kept in the house.

We were locked into what was really a philosophical war — no minor marital disagreement. M.D. was convinced that reason would triumph over dog and fear; the Islanders thought otherwise. So did I, and finally told him he would have to choose between the hopelessly irrational majority and the potentially sensible dog. While he was debating how to solve this acute problem, a notice was posted up on the ferry below the one forbidding the consumption of liquor while at sea: "No dogs are to be taken into the cabin. If it is necessary to transport them, they must be securely tied up on the deck."

A lot of talk about us and the Dalmatian had forced the Captain to promulgate this new law. I still feel guilty when I see some harmless little mutt tied up and shivering on the rear deck, icy spray drenching it during a winter crossing. Laws are more easily made than rescinded. As the battle raged on, week after week, I sometimes fleetingly remembered the simple Romanesque charm of a tiny church in the Tarn, its impressive stone altar. "That's where they put a chair, got a Goddess of Reason to climb up and sit on it during the revolution," the ancient sacristan, decades ago, said as he rattled on about the history of the place. His grandfather had told him she was reputed to be the village beauty at that time, a gorgeous girl, "fit to be worshipped." How simplified life would be if one were enlightened, I thought; but then, sad addendum, maybe that lovely goddess found village living just as complicated as usual when she jumped down from the altar?

In the end, reluctantly and still rather puzzled by the vagaries of human — and animal — nature, M.D. advertised for a country home for the Dalmatian. I pitied the hopeful people who took it away, seduced by its youthful beauty. And I sorrowed for defeated M.D., who I knew had a double interest in the matter, physiological as well as philosophical. Apparently, of all dogs, only Dalmatians excrete uric acid as humans do, which makes them uniquely interesting to a pathologist. (Birds have the same gift, I gather, but they were not involved in our insular problem, thank God.) The dog disappeared beyond the horizon and we were rapidly forgiven as new scandals erupted on the Island to take over its star billing. The present situation was obviously more complex, mysterious, I realised as we docked.

Over the weekend, the explanation surfaced and at first sight, there was no simple solution to a grave difficulty. Pat, next door, came over early on Saturday morning, all agog with the news — just the sort that he loves to retail with considerable dramatic detail. He was so excited that he didn't stop to take off his boots, just clumped right into the kitchen.

A Treasured Island

Pat never speaks quietly or circumspectly, never sits at the table and looks out to sea when visiting; that Saturday his voice was urgently loud as he stood there.

"You mean to say you ain't heard what happened?" Nobody had said a word to us on the boat, so how could we have heard?

"Well…" He drew a deep breath, delighted to be the first to inform us. Sometimes it is easy to give pleasure, merely by listening.

"Monday evening I helped Jerry move his stuff down from the parsonage. Didn't take long — there weren't much to carry. He seemed pleased enough with the house and I made sure he lit the stove right before I went home. But he kept the lights on awful late that night. Same thing Tuesday night, but I ain't seen him that day nor the next. Then, Wednesday night, when Mum and Leonard and me was watching T.V., there came a hammering on the door. Jerry was there, white as a sheet and shaking like a leaf. 'What's come over you boy?' says Mum. 'It's a ghost,' says Jerry, and he told us all about it. So we had him sleep here the rest of the week."

Pat paused before pronouncing judgment. "They all say it was a cruel thing to do — to take a boy into the house like that and not *warn* him — and him all alone. He could of died of fright, being a mainlander and not knowing nothing about Jacob."

* * *

I stayed on the Island when M.D. went back to work on Monday and was cooking a supper for two when Jerry got back after school. As we ate, he gradually answered my questions with perfect matter-of-factness.

"What happened?" he said nonchalantly, chewing sausages and mash, looking out over the little bay. (I always sit in the chair at the stove-end of Jacob's table. This leaves the full sea-view for guests; and I am close to the stove-top from which our meals are directly served.)

"Well, the Monday night I got my supper and then I sat down at the kitchen table to do my homework. It was a still night, everything quiet — no wind at all. And then, the cups hanging by the sink began to swing on their hooks and bump into each other; I thought they'd break. Sounds silly, I know. But I couldn't figure it out... Then I went to my room to fetch some more paper and at the top of the stairs I suddenly went icy cold, all over, and I saw the door to the big attic open wide and then close all by itself. The only sound was the latch clicking. I felt strange but I went all over the house looking to see if one of the boys had got in and was playing tricks on me. Nobody there but when I was in the parlour I could swear the yellow eyes of that old owl followed me. Back in the kitchen, I saw that another chair had been pulled up to the table and the coldness came over me again."

Jerry did not sleep well that night nor the next, and was glad to leave for school in the morning. He did not tell anyone about his fears but by Wednesday evening, he scarcely had the courage to go into the house. When he heard a door creak in the attic and slow footsteps on the stairs as he began his homework, he gave up and ran next door.

Pat, of course, filled him in with the long history of Jacob's haunting. A dozen people had seen the old fellow staring out of the little window; *everybody* knew he was still in the house.

I enquired what made Jerry so certain that he wasn't

imagining things, that Pat was right.

"That's easy. I told my Dad about it over the weekend and he said the proof was that dreadful cold feeling that came over me. Then he told me what to do." Pause — a few more mouthfuls of supper for the fresh-faced growing boy before the simple anti-ghost recipe. "You just light a candle, take out your Bible and read from it; you'll have no more trouble with bad spirits." The lad, still in clean jeans (his Mum must do his laundry in town, I surmised), was now confident he could cope with any sort of ghostly intrusion.

"You won't mind being alone in the house any more?" I was astonished; here was a boy who believed his father implicitly, which is rare these days; rarer still, perhaps, the father believed the son.

Over the apple pie, the conversation turned to other matters.

"Do you believe in rapture?" Jerry asked with polite interest — obviously a well-brought-up boy, if an odd question. And then, emphatically: "I do."

"Oh, I do too" I said brightly before I realised that his rapture had a capital R, which made it different from my humble and fleeting experiences of unmitigated joy. Jerry's Rapture was what would happen when the Apocalypse finally hit. At that moment, whatever they might be doing at the time, Jerry and his Dad and all the other deserving believers, would be snatched up into heaven, leaving unwashed dishes in sinks, cows half-milked, planes short a pilot, trains and cars charging around without their holy drivers. It was a frightening scenario and I began to wonder how many of the ferry crew had been "saved." Might a boatload of sinful passengers, including us, be left to drift out into the Atlantic on our own? This question I did not put to Jerry; enough that he and his father fortunately colluded in their faith, or their credulity. Orwell says they are not the same thing; but who knows which is which? Plenty of highly intelligent people in this century alone seem to have believed implicitly in some earthly utopia or other; but even in my youth I could not go along happily with Plato, Marx, H.G. Wells, Shaw, Lenin, the good Webbs, nor with their capitalist or corporate or rationalist enemies and even less these days with the latest psychological or technological gurus. A lifetime at sea; and not on the waters of the Sea of Tranquillity. (Where is that, anyhow? On the moon, I rather think, which would be a suitable place for it, at least until recently.) Jerry had cheerfully chosen a posthumous paradise, others plump for re-incarnation, a sort of eminently reasonable, "if at first you don't succeed, try, try and try again" philosophy quite without appeal to me because it seemed so dismal. You are miserable now, or an "untouchable," are you? Well, that's what you deserve; you were obviously wicked once, some centuries ago. On Tuesday morning, anyway, I sailed for the mainland worry-free, convinced that the problem of Jacob, if not of Rapture, was solved.

Being an ingenious boy, Jerry decided after a week or two of thoroughly effective candle-lighting and Bible-reading, that he could save time and get on with his homework better if he painted a suitable picture. This labour-saving device was an impressively realistic work of art; the candle, straight and true in the simple glass candlestick, shed a golden light on the opened pages of the Good Book. Jerry framed it and kept it beside him while he did his homework and when he went to bed. The last we heard of the painter was that he had gone out West and was doing very well as a graphic artist.

* * *

Ours was an accommodating ghost; his rapid disappearance and the consequent contentment of our human lodger also meant that we were rapidly re-instated as trustworthy Islanders. Within weeks, old Jacob's short-lived stardom was forgotten as further problems loomed to occupy many minds. Other people, over the years, have suffered far more.

Martin, the invaluable supplier of old mulching hay for my vegetable garden, is one of them. Each spring he loaded the bales, which had already done five months duty as winter insulation banked around his cottage, into his small tractor and puttered over here. Together, we forked the hay into a pile on the garden, ready for spreading between the rows of seedlings as they emerged; he said he had no use for the stuff for which I was so grateful, might as well give it to me as chuck it over the cliff. He keeps no animals to feed it to nowadays; when he had a few cows he gave me manure as well. I have a feeling he thinks I am mildly mad but humours me anyhow; no other woman on the Island has developed a mulching-habit. They all say that the hay brings in weed seeds, I maintain it keeps them down and also keeps the soil moist in drought summers. I had been easily converted by a pleasant woman who, some decades ago, earned the happy title: "The Mother of Mulch." Her brother Rex Stout was even more famous, as a writer of detective stories. The man succeeded, lucratively, no doubt, in a comparatively new literary genre, the woman merely resurrected a quite recently forgotten dictum of rural common sense, familiar to me from a European childhood. But the attitude of the Island women was understandable; most of them are now cultivating plots of land which are small compared with the one Jacob left us. There is no room for mulch between their crowded rows of vegetables, nor to allow a few square yards to lie fallow for a year.

For me, in any case, until his great barn, and the haymaker with it, burnt down one recent night and there was nothing more to bring over, hay-day was always an eagerly awaited date on my calendar — Martin delivering a sure sign of a new spring, Martin with a few more good tales to tell. He hardly ever comes visiting at the kitchen table, prefers to talk in the open air.

He brought the hay late one year, mid May. It had been a long, hard winter. There was still some frost lingering in the ground. By the time we had forked all the bales, we were quite hot and I, quite breathless. Martin climbed back up onto his tractor but made no move to start the motor; the need to talk had come over him.

Martin lived with his wife and children in a very small and rather shabby old cottage — shabby by the high standards of most Islanders on the loop road. It stood at the crest of a long strip of land stretching to the shore and was surrounded by at least a dozen out-buildings, each of which one might say had been "purpose-built." Now that the sheep and fattening calves were gone, time left over from fishing, he occupied himself tinkering in one or other of them. The children were gradually disappearing to the mainland; although the odd grandchild turned up to be looked after most kindly by his wife.

"Don't take long to hoard a pile o' junk, yer know," said Martin from his hard metal seat above me. I was looking at the land, the soil spread last fall with seaweed. The subterranean activity was almost audible — seeds of wild poppies, johnny-jump-ups, even stray petunias and columbines, as well as weeds, all sprouting bravely, liberated from their frozen prison, together with a myriad of tiny creatures, some good, some evil, from my prejudiced point of view. The great resurrection had begun.

"Junk..." I agreed with Martin. "Once you've begun, there's no way to stop." We had already put up four extra buildings — workshop and garage for machinery, boathouse and winery, summerhouse or gazebo and tool shed, woodshed — and all are filled to overflowing. The wood can be burned but what on earth will our children do with the rest of the stuff — ours and Jacob's and his father's — when we die? Perhaps we should put a codicil to our wills, leaving it all to Martin to enrich his own store? It would please him, I know he can never fully gratify his passion for junk. It is an addiction, really, but an innocent and reasonable one since, on an island, if you can't lay your hand on the right length of timber, the correct nut and bolt, or the missing tractor part when you need it, you can't go round the corner and shop for it. Martin's huge barn, which is probably even older than his house — all mortised and tenoned, not a nail in it — is a cathedral of junk. The last time I was in it, hoping to borrow something or other, the rosy light of a setting sun filtered through the dusty loft windows and bathed the shelves neatly piled with old car-springs, rusty tools and fishing-gear, willow baskets and half-empty cans of paint. It was curiously peaceful and orderly, reflecting a hidden side of Martin, who in his person was quite dishevelled. He had created a temple to the "waste not, want not" philosophy of an earlier time. Meeting him casually, one might not think him capable of such an achievement; his faded blue eyes darted all over the place, his jaws were seldom still as he chewed his gum, nor was his tongue, out of doors, anyhow. He told me once that his "nerves" were shot years ago when, as a young man, he went out West briefly to work in a B.C. lumber camp; they have never recovered properly. But that is another supernatural story, which concerns vampire bats, one of which attacked him as he slept. Here on the Island we only have the charming little ones; they sometimes slip into the house and flit around in marvellous silence, but never bite you in the throat.

The story Martin told me now from up on his tractor was more immediate. It was in the great barn that the haunting began. He was tinkering away in there at dusk one fall evening when he heard the door being snibbed from the outside. It was a while before a son discovered him and let him out. "Strange, but nothing to worry about," he thought, until he noticed he was no longer alone as he went about his daily chores.

"A person knows when 'e ain't alone, don't 'e?"

I nodded.

"Well," he went on, looking over my head to the spruce woods up on the point, "somebody or something took to following me around when I went to see to the sheep or whatever."

"Did you ever catch sight of anybody or anything?" I asked.

"No, I ain't never set eyes on 'im, because 'e was always behind me and I don't 'ave no eyes in the back of me head. But I seen the cat's hair stand on end when she were in the barn with me, an' I seen my junk had been moved about when I weren't looking, an' I got locked into one or other of my buildings time and time again. Twice 'e got into the house and I 'eard footsteps on the stairs to Janey's room."

I did not ask whether "he" had actually entered this teen-aged daughter's bedroom.

Martin's lost eyes came back to me.

"After a while, I began to wonder. Maybe what was bothering me was a ghost from one of them foreign boats that went down in the bay in times past. Maybe 'e's after getting buried properly. Or 'e might be an old Viking — they say those fellows came to these parts…couldn't do no harm to try and bury 'im, put 'im to rest, anyhow, like I said to Pat, and maybe it'd be a kindness."

So Pat joined Martin in the woods one afternoon and helped him dig a good-sized grave. The ghost gratefully slipped into it right away; he had, of course, followed the men as they chose a likely resting place for him.

"Didn't 'ave to do a thing," said Martin, "'e knew what we were about. I could feel that 'e was quiet, happy-like, as soon as 'e got in — it was like a big weight off of me, all of a sudden."

The two men filled in the long hole with the loose soil and walked back through the woods with their spades over their shoulders, content with a job well done. There was no more haunting, even though the grave was disturbed a few days after the burial.

Lester was back in those same woods, working on a road he is aiming to cut through the trees to a bit of beach he owns when he noticed it. He was puzzled. In the old days, as Neighbour told me, they buried you where you dropped. (A small visiting granddaughter enquired, interrupting our confidential chat then by asking, "But suppose you died in the kitchen?") Now, in any case, and for more than a hundred and fifty years, we have a proper graveyard up by the church.

The thought came into Lester's head that some mainlander, over for a day or two, had been up to mischief. Perhaps there had been a fight, a murder even, and the murderer buried the body under the trees where he thought it would never be found? Lester went back for his tractor with the bucket on it and dug up the grave. He was still puzzled when he found it empty.

It had served its purpose as far as Martin was concerned, anyhow.

"But yer know," he said, "after all them years with 'im, I sometimes misses 'im now. 'E was company…" He started up the motor and chugged off back to his little house and his many outbuildings.

* * *

I, too, have my ghosts. Somebody said one should choose one's ghosts as one chooses one's friends — with care. I like to think I selected mine judiciously, one at a time, over the years; but perhaps, like Martin's, they chose me. They inhabit the green space up on the headland which I call the Dell. Looking to the west through the trunks of the spruces there one can see the glint of the ocean, catch the murmur of the waves.

The difference between Martin's ghost and mine is chiefly due to my knowing somewhat more about mine than he does about his, despite his long familiarity with the drowned mariner; I can read the letters and books they wrote, study their features in old portraits, so that each at least has an identity, even while remaining as mysterious in death as they were in life. And, of course, having each other for company, mine seldom come down the hill to the house or the buildings; but if they do not need me, I need them. I resent the elements when the snow is too deep or the rain too heavy to allow me to follow the rough path up to the Dell.

Chapter 5

The Making of Gardens

*I have seen flowers come in stony places,
And kind things done by men with ugly faces...*
— John Masefield

The laying out of a vegetable garden is a rational undertaking, brain-work, and left-brain at that, aided by the due amount of muscle-work. Vigilance in forestalling the lively crowd of hopeful predators, bacterial, insect or animal, and generosity in supplying suitable nourishment will almost guarantee an orderly harvest, year after year, given well-fed soil like ours.

A flower garden is another matter altogether — a mad endeavour, perhaps pointless, never completed, never mastered, endlessly uplifting and constantly humbling.

I determined, nevertheless, to create one on a memorable July day four years after we became Islanders. By then, the house was more than habitable and we were growing enough vegetables on the cliff-top plot to supply not only ourselves but sundry mainland households. It was time for a grander vision to take over, and it came to me as I sat on the upper deck of the little ferry sailing home. The sea was serene, the sun warm and the gentlest of breezes was blowing off the Island. Quite suddenly, about a mile from shore, the boat was enveloped in a heady cloud of flower fragrances

— wild roses, wild phlox, unknown other blossoms. We sailed through it for ten full minutes. There was a mile-wide scented fringe to the west of the Island that evening; I knew that, by the next summer, flowers that I must grow would be adding to its unexpected presence. And the house itself would be lapped in its own cloud of fragrance, wherever the breeze might be blowing from.

* * *

When we first arrived, the cottage and its out-buildings stood waist-deep in tall hay. After much scything and mowing, we had now achieved a sort of lawn — a very distant relation to a city lawn, but green, and interesting, if one studied it. The area at the foot of the wooded hill was a carpet of wild strawberries, other parts were almost entirely dandelions, elsewhere known as "pissenlits" because thought to be a good diuretic, used here merely for wine-making and spring greens, or buttercups and other self-seeding or creeping plants. Civilised grass grew only where we had dug up the sod to lay a pipe from the well and to put in a septic system on the steep slope from the house to the shore — work which required seeding afterwards.

Where on our green acres should I plant my first flowers? Somewhere protected from the almost constant winds, where the sun would shine on them most of the day, where the soil, explored by the heavy iron pry bar Jacob had left us, did not seem too thin over the bedrock... The only such place, behind the house, was already bespoken; it was a miniature orchard in which we had planted five dwarf fruit trees.

Through the long winter nights, I dreamed of all the gardens I had ever known, each with its own atmosphere and scents: the broad herbaceous border in southern England, exuberant all summer long with phlox, lupins and big clumps of Michaelmas daisies, the mountain-side one in North Vancouver where the blue delphiniums grew head-high and begonias flourished under the evergreen trees, the orderly pattern of bright beds in the one in southern France, the classical Italian ones. Memories of all these and more flooded through me; and none could be re-created with the simple tools and middle-aged muscles at my disposal — and the salt wind blowing unrelentingly for at least a few hours every day.

The solution to the dilemma came serendipitously, as a result of our desire to restore the house to its original shape.

* * *

While Jacob was still sharing the cottage with his offspring, a small wing had been tacked onto the west wall, obscuring the view of the sun as it flamed and sank over the sea. We decided to cut it off and move it elsewhere to serve as a shed; the large living-room we had created by tearing down the walls of two smaller rooms would then be lit by both the rising and the setting sun, while the tall north windows continued to frame the busy life of the bay. But how were we to tackle so complicated an operation?

Consulted by M.D., William came down to look the situation over, pronounced it a simple matter, volunteered to take charge, and set a date. We had, it seemed, presented him with the sort of small engineering challenge he most enjoys.

Heavy May rain was falling on the appointed morning, but William appeared punctually with the four men he had lined up for the job, all in waders and yellow oilskins, and work began in a methodical manner; William, with his long experience and ingenious mind, could captain a crew on land as well as aboard a ship, without himself lifting a finger. He harbours a belief that each child is born into this world with its own particular and finite store of energy; when that store is exhausted, the person dies. Now that he was approaching old age, he was increasingly concerned not to over-exert himself, noticing his own vitality running low. (These days, at around eighty, he even drives, in whichever of his ancient vehicles happens to be in running order, the two hundred yards from his house to his wharf on his almost daily tours of inspection; although, once there, he is apt to forget himself and take a heavy maul to a loose timber or shovel shingle behind the low sea-wall.)

Obeying the Captain's succinct orders, the crew now man-handled limbed tree-trunks into place while M.D. clambered up on the roof with his chain-saw. Within ten minutes, he had cut the wing free of the house, and it was ready to be heaved onto the rollers with a jack, shifted ten feet sideways and then pulled back twenty-five. Daniel chugged up with perfect timing on his little tractor to help with these last manoeuvres, ropes and pulleys were attached in accordance with the Captain's directions, and the move began, gently, a couple of feet with each tug of the tractor. By noon, the building stood straight and true on its new foundations — a slab of rock under each corner. All it wanted was a fourth wall, which we hammered on a day or two later.

Dripping wet, but plainly satisfied with their work, William, Daniel, and the crew trooped into the kitchen, shed their oilskins, and accepted a few beers round the kitchen table — the only payment they wished for their time and labour. Ours was only partially a money economy, there was still, to some extent, a survival system of barter from the old days when cash was almost non-existent. Neighbour, telling me tales of the past, has pointed out that the Islanders scarcely noticed the Great Depression of the 'thirties; they had no money to lose.

When the men, full of good cheer, donned their rain-garb again and went on their way, I put on mine. Standing there surveying the new lie of the land, it dawned on me that the first flower garden had chosen its own perfect site, sheltered from the winds by the new shed to the north and the hill to the south, basking in the day-long sun, slightly sloped for good drainage. That summer we dug a wide half-moon out of the sod, pried out innumerable huge rocks, added loads of rotted sawdust from behind the old boat-shop in the South Cove, and I began to plant.

Word had, of course, flown around the Island about what we were up to, and by the fall the women were dropping by with roots of perennials from their own gardens or little pokes of seeds they had saved for me. They would be back the following summer to exclaim with pleasure over the young display. The traditional division of labour here dictates that the men grow the potatoes and cabbages and the women are in charge of everything else — herbs, vegetables, flowers — and most of them take great pride in their work.

Sir Thomas More's Utopia, at two hundred miles across, was a huge island compared with our tiny dot on the map, and it was inhabited by marvellously orderly citizens who would have been shocked by the often eccentric ways of our small population. One thing, however, besides the encircling sea, we still share with them — a lingering passion for gardens.

"They set great store by [them]," wrote the saint. "In them they have vineyards, all manner of fruit, herbs and flowers, so pleasant, so well-furnished and so finely kept, that I never saw anything more fruitful nor better trimmed in any place." Some of our old gardens and orchards are abandoned now that the population has dwindled, but many still come up to Utopian standards, and the ardent flower-lovers seemed glad to find in me a new, if ignorant, recruit to their number.

M.D.'s passport to acceptance by the community was his working background; he had brought no tools of his trade with him to the Island but could still be called upon for First Aid at the scene of an accident or advice at an old person's bedside as to whether the ferry should be called upon to make a mercy run to the mainland. He was an unexpected gift to the Islanders, and they were grateful. In my case, more time was required, enough to see whether I could, and would, dig and hoe and cause things to grow. I waited, perforce, and was rewarded.

* * *

The shed soon settled down in its new position. I planted narrow perennial beds on two of its sides, a climbing rose on the south wall, and two honeysuckles, gift of Neighbour's mother, on the east. She cut me pieces from a sprawling old bush by her back door; now they cover the whole wall, and hummingbirds hover there on invisible wings each June, sipping nectar.

The first flower-garden was still in its infancy when fate pushed me on into evermore ambitious schemes. A simple thought, an idle question, and the die is cast.

***

"Do you think William might have any ideas on getting rid of those brambles?" I asked M.D. over soup-lunch one day. Every time I went down to weed the vegetables I was irked by an extensive, and spreading, area of wild and prickly shrubs. It interrupted the sweep of the lawn, but we had been unable to tame it, let alone scythe it or mow it.

Consulted again, William stroked his chin for a minute or two and then announced happily:

"You know, I always had a mind to make a flame-thrower. And it just might do the trick. Worth a try, anyhow."

Two days later, the thing in William's mind had become a welded contraption with a long pipe protruding from it. Neighbour put aside her sewing and came down to stand with us and watch the crucial trial.

It worked all right, in that a glorious flame leapt from the mouth of the pipe with a muffled roar — and nothing exploded. But, sadly, although leaves shrivelled in the heat, the stems and branches of the matted brambles seemed impervious to the assault. A major forest fire might have done the trick, but nothing less fierce.

Only mildly disappointed, William returned to his workshop to perfect his next invention, a gadget for keeping the gulls off his big boathouse on the beach. They have a habit of perching in a row along the peak, twenty or thirty at a time, and their droppings are said to rot the roofing. Every island breeds its Crusoes; there are more than a dozen here.

Fortunately, fate stepped in almost at once. I took the binoculars from the kitchen window-sill to "spy" the wharf as the ferry docked a week later, thinking a mainland friend might be aboard. (In every house around the bay "spy-glasses" sit waiting by a sea-ward window: we like to know who is going and coming, whose boat has just tied up and how low in the water it is with the catch, what sail that is out to sea.)

Instead of the expected friend, I watched a majestic back-hoe lumber off the ferry. It turned out that it had crossed the water to dig a couple of cellars for new houses to be built by young couples, and to do some work on our decrepit road. The burly owner and driver of the machine was an old friend of William's — and so it came about that our intractable bramble patch was metamorphosed into a sunken rose garden.

At noon, a couple of days later, I noticed the enormous machine parked up the hill. Neighbour was serving Roland a fish chowder, accompanied by talk of other times, when he had been lighthouse keeper on another island. When William brought him down to survey the thorny problem after lunch, Roland took a quick look and strode right back up the hill to get his machine.

"A half-hour," he called back over his shoulder, "and she'll be finished."

The bramble patch, I had realised long since, was actually the site of an ancient barn. "Fell down around 1920," said William; and indeed Roland uncovered two rows of massive foundation rocks, half-buried in the ground.

"Where'll we put 'em?"

Quick decision called for, as the growling machine nosed around them impatiently.

"Push them out in a big circle," I shouted above the roar, and tried to indicate the suitable periphery by walking round about fifteen feet from the middle of the patch.

Within forty-five minutes Roland and his magnificent machine had done their work. Eight vast rocks lay at peace like sleeping rhinos round the border of my projected rose-garden, and a dozen more, somewhat smaller, had been carefully placed against the curve of the hill where it meets the lawn, thirty feet to the east. These last were the skeleton of the second garden Roland gave me that afternoon — a rockery. It was a day on which I blessed modern technology.

But Roland, a wise and meditative man, was master of his machine; much of the time these days it is the machine which masters us. Here, where fishing kept the community alive for two hundred years, we know what horrors too clever machinery can cause; the great draggers have scoured the ocean, taken what they wanted, vomited the rest, and left our people with an almost empty sea. And it has happened within the fifteen or so years since Roland's kindness gave me such joy. Now I stand amongst my fragrant roses and look out on an ocean which, despite its blue and restless beauty, is dying.

*　*　*

For two winters after Roland's visit I worked on the Wall — not Hadrian's, nor the Great One of China, nor any other construction designed to keep people, or even animals, in or out. My Wall's simple mission was to protect the future roses from the cruel force of an on-shore gale. The Island is as rich in rocks as it is in many other necessities of life. I gathered them from the hill, where they seem to grow in clumps like plants, and made forays to the beach from time to time. When they were too heavy for one woman to lift, I took to a stone-chisel and mallet to reduce them to a reasonable size. Much of our rock is shale, which was designed by the Almighty to give joy to rock-splitters. Few moments in life are more satisfying than those in which a great slab of rock answers to the deftly placed chisel, the

The Making of Gardens

smart tap of the mallet, and falls open with a small, complaining sound of protest.

Around the bay, the women "spied" me from their windows, slowly adding stone to stone, filling in the gaps between the giant rocks placed so judiciously by Roland. Gradually they saw a steady wall with a good batter rise from the ground to a height of four or five feet. Some of them wondered whether I had gone mad, trudging around in the snow and ice, lugging rocks down from the hill or up from beach; but I knew it was a sane occupation.

Two winters' work to complete the Wall, one spring's work to fetch sea-smoothed flat stones from the beach on the other side of the Island for a little patio at one end of the sunken garden — a sheltered place to sit and contemplate — and to lay out yin and yang beds between curving gravel paths, the mathematics and the concrete curbs supplied by M.D.'s ingenuity, and it was time to plant. "Lilli Marlene," a throbbing deep red filled the yang, "Pernille Poulsen," a subtly shaded pink the yin — German and Danish roses quite at home here — and finally three native "New Dawn," rambling with abandon around the inside of the Wall.

* * *

"Something there is," said Robert Frost, appropriately, "that doesn't love a wall." I suppose he had been tramping round New England walled fields one spring and noticed some disarray among the stones, the result of the silent winter heaving of the frozen land. Something there is, however, that does love a rock wall with passion — the multitude of mice who share the land with us.

In the house, October is mouse-month. As the days shorten, they slip in invisibly and begin to set up suitably warm winter quarters. Tradition dies hard with them, as with some of us, and they harbour an ancestral memory of the easy days when the cottage stood empty of interfering humans, and the only predator within its walls, the old owl, was stuffed and glass-eyed, and then of the even better ones after our advent, which added food to shelter. The first autumn of our tenancy we found a nest in our bed; since then I have gradually taken measures to claim our territory, and by November, normally, the mice have gracefully accepted defeat and retreated.

Is it the same mice which have wintered for years now under the Wall in carefully constructed underground galleries, made accessible through neat holes in the sod around the sunken garden? These settlements having proved satisfactory winter quarters, the pioneers went on to colonise the rockery not far away, with unexpectedly valuable results from my point of view. Plainly, whoever they are, they enjoy a rock roof over their dwellings.

When I tried to be scientific about rodents (not really my field), I realised that the subterranean settlers under the wall and the rockery were probably what we call here "Land Mice," who are much bigger and stronger than my dainty little house or field-mice, which are similar to Burns' "wee sleekit, cow'rin, tim'rous, beasties" whose plans, like ours, "gang aft a'gley." They have unpleasantly long snouts, and look more closely related to rats, creatures which never themselves reached the Island despite the many ships sunk in our waters. I can only suppose that the refugees I unkindly chased from the house each fall died of inanition in the bitter winter weather; but how did enough of them survive to invade us the following October? Another unanswered query to take to my grave.

The Making of Gardens

Roses, if they enjoy their surroundings (and what rose would not love the peaceful pool of sunlight afforded by the Wall?) behave generously and predictably. But a rockery is a Darwinian struggle for survival. The Wall completed, I had embarked on filling in the gaps between the big rocks laid by Roland against the sloping land with smaller stones, pockets of good soil, and finally plants.

Up the hill, where one of the meandering paths leads to the Dell, the ground is covered with creeping junipers of different sorts, amicably woven together to form a springy carpet of varying greens. How on earth did they arrive up here, in this wilderness of bayberries, ferns, wild roses and raspberries, I wondered; and wonder still. Dark green, light green, a feathery blue-green — roots of each took well amongst the rocks, an evergreen backbone for my planting. Heather from the cliff-top and a silvery plant from the beach joined them, and then, word having run around the Island about my new scheme, the flowers flowed in.

Neighbour's mother gave me pieces of snow-in-summer; Mary, newly widowed and tidying up house and garden, stopped me one day as I went to the store and pressed roots of purple bugles on me; Ella came over with some aubretia — and so it went until there were fifteen or more different plants flowering, each in its own moment, beginning as soon as the birds, confident that spring would indeed arrive, began nest-building. First, lifting the heart after the long winter, the clumps of primulas Neighbour brought, then the low rounded mound of the native rhododendron at the back, the woolly thyme thick with minute mauve flowers — and bees — foaming cascades of the fragrant snow-in-summer. Every week or two new colours to surprise, new scents, and when the blooms died in September with the last pale hostas and pink sedums, the silver foliage and evergreens still clothed the rocks gracefully.

For two or three years, everything was orderly, balanced, discreetly perfect in the blend of colour and growth over the rocks. As I came up from the vegetable garden each day, I would stand for a minute or two and admire.

Now, however, years later, maturity has taken its toll. When I survey the rockery these days, I see a wild tangle of plants spilling over and obscuring the stones, intermingling with each other with a total disregard for my plans, each one out to take over its neighbour's territory, and the more adventurous ones questing out into the lawn beyond them.

It is a salutary and humbling sight, and one to be expected in old age. The rockery could be my old woman's mind; long ago it seemed to be controlled and clear about what mattered, now it is a thicket of uncertainties, a patchwork of incoherent conclusions about the history I have lived through, the preceding centuries, and what is to come. Age, someone observed, makes one either bigoted or confused. Could it be both?

Brave young thoughts, like some of the indomitable plants, appear unexpectedly from time to time, amidst the tangle, and so do curious memories which have no right to life. I no longer try to cultivate the rockery or the mind — both must go their own way.

* * *

It is the mice who prevent total madness amongst the slabs of stone these days in the rockery. Since they overflowed from their habitations under the Wall, their burrows among these other rocks keep the most rampant plants in check as they nibble on their roots.

The Making of Gardens

I could do with a few small rodents to trim up my muddled mind.

* * *

It is not, of course, merely mental clutter which is a problem. There is also the matter of connections between thoughts and places, names and faces. In the old head thoughts and names slip around corners. You know they are hiding there, just out of reach, but can't entice them out into the open; they only show themselves again if you stop hunting — often twenty seconds of being ignored is all it takes to lure them out.

They say now, the experts, that faces and names are filed in separate parts of the brain, which accounts for the difficulty of matching them. The infant, after all, only needs to know his mother's face: her name can have no importance to him for several years, and when he finally learns it, it is tucked away in another corner of his mind, labelled "names." But the experts have not simplified the disposition of thoughts and memories so easily, nor of rampant plants.

One odd memory haunts me still whenever I leave the house or the vegetable garden ("kitchen gardens" we used to call such plots in England sixty years ago, and they do indeed demand a certain drudgery) to tend the roses whose happiness here I owe to Daniel, William and Roland. Even a rose can be lethal, I learnt from an old medical textbook of the 1930s A tragic case-history of murder by a rose-bush gave details of the fate of a young woman who loved her rose garden, and a clinical photograph of the patient on her death-bed accompanied the medical story. Her abundant black hair was spread out around her lovely face, which was as white as the pillow she lay on; but her lips were slightly parted in the "risus sardonicus," the wide involuntary smile caused by muscle spasms in the last stages of the brief disease. She had contracted it, the pathologists said, when one of her cherished rose-bushes pricked her. I have been pricked a thousand times, especially by the old roses, which are better armoured than the less independent modern ones, but have gratefully survived. No tetanus, and no rats bearing cholera, or plague on this little Island, it seems, just mice.

Chapter 6

Harry

Animals are such agreeable friends —
they ask no questions, they pass no criticisms.
— George Eliot

A slender young moon lay on her back as she slipped up the still sky the other night. I lay on mine and watched from my bed through the tall west window.

Angels can fly, I heard from a very heavy man named Chesterton, because they take themselves lightly. The angel who flies above the gazebo was briefly at rest — and so was I. This one has blown her horn into every shifting wind, every boisterous gale, for years now, and miraculously shows no signs of weariness. On a moonlit night she is transformed into gleaming silver, her simple earthly origins forgotten; she was designed by our artist-daughter, cut from base metal by M.D., and is the only weathervane on the Island. The fishermen have no need of such a thing — they know in their bones about the winds and the water. She is also the only angel; the old wooden church up the hill is plain and unadorned, and never speaks of such messengers from heaven. But I am grateful for the unfailing information she brings me, lonely as she may feel on this rocky shore.

The angel instructs me about the weather, the Islanders who come to visit at our kitchen table teach me other things.

A Treasured Island

Even before Pat from next door barged in with his concerns about Jacob's ghost so soon after our arrival, old Harry was on the doorstep. He knew exactly when we had signed the deed and had been watching impatiently for our arrival. He had a scheme in mind and no time to lose in putting it into operation.

As he sat at the table, his watery old eyes on the water below us, we realised we had met him before, on the July day we first took the boat from the mainland to look the cottage over. After exploring the house, the barns and their contents, bemused by what we had seen, we walked up the path to the woods and the headland; we knew that these twenty-five acres were part of the property. The ground was rough and mossy in the green shade of the spruces, but shortly we stepped out into a wide smooth meadow on the cliff-top, flooded with sunlight.

Hay-making was in progress: old Harry, lean and a bit bent, his slip of a wife, in a cotton dress and sun-bonnet, and their brawny son, Herb, were forking up the hay onto the high wagon. When they became aware of strangers on their land, the little group stood still, eyeing us from a distance. The splendid yoke of oxen in the traces did not seem interested.

After some moments of silent appraisal, Harry walked over to investigate us more closely. We were relieved to see that our explanation of what we were doing on the Island interested him; he beckoned to Milly and Herb to join us. So, standing there with the smell of hay pleasant on the sea air, we became acquainted with our first Island friends.

They wanted to know what we thought of Jacob's place, if we really meant to buy it at the exorbitant price his children were asking for it — one which seemed to us mainlanders ridiculously cheap and actually within our means — and what we wanted to live on the Island for, anyway.

"Well," said M.D., "we always wanted to live by the sea and we never could. Too many children, too much work… And now we're getting older; if we don't make a move soon, it'll be too late."

Harry nodded his head, and so did Milly. It seemed a good enough answer.

"You'd best know, if that's the way it is," said Harry, looking hard at us, "that you can't trust everyone you'll meet here."

Then the three of them began a litany of warnings about the land and the people who think they have a claim on some of it, because Jacob's father had grabbed more than he had a right to a hundred years ago, and hung onto it, despite all the feuding.

We knew from the beginning that there was another twenty acres which came with the twenty-five the house stood on. They are scattered all over the Island; it was to take us several years to find all the odd-shaped parcels. And we did in fact come to grief several times through our ignorance. In buying the house and land, we had also bought its bitter history. Once, when we gave away a tiny piece on which someone wanted to keep his vehicle and gear, there was a tremendous fuss. It was not ours to give, some people said, and one of the old men stopped us on the way to the store, and warned us, quite kindly, but very firmly:

"Never meddle with the land. You don't know enough about it — it'll just make trouble." Deuteronomy (27:17) quite a while ago told us that "he that removeth his neighbour's landmark" would be cursed. We were beginning to get hints that there had been plenty of cursing over the marks on the small Island acreage over the years.

Simple-minded people, we had thought that our deed and the elaborate four-foot square plan of all our property, surveyed in 1920, gave us rights. We did not realise that not everyone agreed with the fancy surveyor Jacob's father, Samuel, had got over from the mainland, long before the days of a ferry to bring him; and their descendants still don't. Some say the man was drunk when he made the survey — and it is true that we discovered some oddities with regard to angles and compass points when M.D. began trying to find the bits and pieces.

His search was enormously complicated anyhow by the fact that the plan merely indicated the shape of each patch of land and whose property abutted on it — no hint of where it lay with regard to the geography of the Island. It required a great deal of talk — and drink — in barns and kitchens as well as the discovery of remnants of ancient rail fences and blazed line trees as clues to or confirmation of a particular boundary.

All education is a slow process, unfortunately. Pat's old aunt, living in the old family house high up on the hill to the east of the bay, explained to me what went on years ago when there was an attempt to strike a binding boundary between her parents' precious land and their neighbour's property. A great rope, some five inches in diameter, a household necessity in every sea-faring family in those days, was thrown down the hillside at the appropriate angle to mark the just division before stakes were driven in and a rail fence could go up. Pat's aunt, a lively old lady who had spent many years off the Island but had not forgotten how to roof a barn, or, indeed, how to cure a small child of asthma by popping it into the opened belly of a newly slaughtered cow

(Victorian shock-therapy? I wondered; she said it worked for her) told me that she and her brothers obeyed whispered instructions from their parents and surreptitiously slipped the rope a few feet further south before the men put up the fence. Thomas More, Sir or Saint, smile at our Island. You knew there was no possible Utopia, no New Man. I wish the rest of us did; it would save a lot of trouble and bloodshed. And hearsay tells me that when, all those centuries ago, you mounted the rough steps to the platform on which your head was to be chopped off, you maintained your wry sense of humour and asked for help to go up. "For the coming down, I will manage for myself," you sensibly said. So must we all, when there can be no more scheming.

More lately, M.D. and I went with Lester, his widowed mother and her two maiden sisters, all three old women togged out as usual in identical gumboots, denim overalls and floppy hats, to verify the division between his woodlot in the middle of the Island and ours. Together we found the old blazed trees and agreed on the line, and when the work was done Martha said with an astonished smile, "And we never came to blows over it!" Those three sisters in their old age still work their gardens, help each other and even co-operate, although not always easily, with the one grown male in the family, Martha's son; no doubt he brings them firewood for heating their cottage. Food they can get from their beautifully tended vegetable plot. Something else they give each summer to passers-by on their way to the store: a few square yards of their land is always given over to brilliant fragrant phlox and other flowers.

* * *

When Harry came calling two days after our arrival,

however, we did not understand what lay ahead of us as the new landowners; and we had to wait half-an-hour before he came to the point of his visit. But it was a profitable and happy half-hour for us as we learnt a thing or two about his own life and about Jacob.

Harry was nearly eighty. He did not fish any more but he still worked his land. As a child of seven, he had dropped out of the Island school and had no regrets.

"Couldn't see no sense to sittin' in that there schoolroom, shivering, me clothes wet through from getting there in the snow — and there was a lot more of that in them days, up over the fences every year." He preferred to follow the men to the woods, the boat-shops or the fish-stores, watch them, and then join them at work as he saw he could be useful. The child got himself an extensive and well-rounded education; and it was not exclusively practical. A fair amount of philosophy, scientific observation, even of poetry goes into building a wooden boat or keeping a family fed from a small patch of rocky land. Later on, I recognised the truth in the words of a young Yukon Indian man who had left the North to go to university. He graduated well, but later went home, and said sensibly: "There are other ways to get educated than through the three R's. There are also the three L's — Look, Listen and Learn, which is what my father did, and his father before him." And Harry.

He had seen many changes in the last thirty or forty years, mostly for the worse, and who knew where it would end? There was talk of closing down the last boatshop, the lobster were getting scarce and, of course, the young people didn't know how to work any more — too much sitting in school or in front of a T.V. But he was grateful that his own young had turned out the way they should; a couple of them often came back to the Island and were good to him and Milly, and of course Herb and his sister still lived here.

A little history, a spot of current affairs, and at last the big question. Harry's old eyes came back from the sea and fixed M.D. (The woman, plainly, would have nothing to say in an important matter like this.)

"Seems to me," he began, "you've got yourself a lot of land and it's maybe more than you'll need. Can't see as you'll be raising animals or putting in cabbages for sauerkraut or savoury — and there'll be enough garden for your kitchen right along where Jacob had his. So the thought came to me that you could be glad to sell a couple of acres…get a bit of your money back…"

Unsure of what he read in M.D.'s face, he went on to explain that the parcel he had in mind lay close to his house near the middle of the Island, just across the road, in fact, and it would be handy for putting three or four young animals on for fattening. And it was, for sure, our land; that was one bit that no one had ever questioned belonged to Jacob, so we *could* sell it. What did M.D. think?

Across the table M.D.'s and my eyes met for an enlightening instant.

"Well," said M.D., "I don't think we're really ready to sell anything. But what would you say to *renting* the land for two or three years — maybe even five?"

Harry surveyed the sea again while we waited and he deliberated. The small waves broke peacefully on the rocks.

"Maybe that'd be all right, if you ain't about to sell. But not for five years — ten years or nothing. No good fixing the fencing unless it's for ten."

"Done," said M.D., and Harry smiled. He still had a fair number of his teeth.

He drove us over in his truck to look at the coveted pasture, and walked us round the perimeter so that there would be no misunderstanding. The next morning he was back at the house again with a year's rent — ten dollars — in his pocket, and made his mark at the bottom of the fine agreement M.D. had concocted for the leasing of the land.

The fence went up rapidly, and four young calves browsed contentedly. Harry was satisfied.

A couple of years later, though, when he came over punctually with the annual rent money, he seemed to be a changed man. Herb had persuaded him to sell his oxen on the mainland and buy a small tractor to do their work.

"I misses them critters something terrible," Harry complained, sitting at the kitchen table again. The loss of Bright and Lion had aged him suddenly and I wondered how many of the ten years of the lease he would enjoy.

"Sometimes," he finished as he left us, "sometimes I thinks I'll get me another pair — just for pets."

He lived a few more years, without any pets. After his death, Milly told me that he was right; the oxen were as gentle as kittens, they understood every word you said to them — even a little bit of a woman like her could handle them. I got the feeling that those great silent animals had been a major bond in the long marriage of their owners.

In the old days the massive creatures would be brought from the mainland, one at a time, in two doreys lashed together, their front legs in one, hind legs in the other, towed by a fish-boat. Contemplative animals, they would calmly voyage to their new home and lumber ashore unruffled. No horse would endure such an experience quietly, so there were never any here; nor were they needed.

Harry's yoke was the last one on the Island. I'm glad we

had a glimpse of them at work before they were displaced by yet another machine.

* * *

They say that an unusual professor at Emporia State University in Kansas wrote these lines:

> *For how can you train a horse to watch cows*
> *if he rides in a trailer all day?*
> *How can you have any worth to your life*
> *if you use a machine to load hay?*

His name was Jim Hoy, and I think he was a cowboy before he got stuck in academe. Harry would have agreed with him, could he have read him.

Chapter 7

Happy Fall

*The creature has a purpose and his eyes
are bright with it.*
— Keats (Letter)

Herb's fall on the icy deck of the ferry fifteen or more years ago was heavy enough to break his leg. He is massive, the strongest man on the Island, they always said, and tall. He and Wes were unloading freight when he suddenly lost his footing. The Captain, William, hearing the shouts, clambered down from the wheel-house; plainly he had an emergency on his hands. Sizing things up, he had the rest of the crew carry Herb, gently, into the cabin, sent word to Ellie by one of the disembarking passengers that there had been a bit of an accident and took the ferry right back to the mainland to find a doctor.

Herb came home a couple of days later with an enormous cast on his left leg, a face drained of its normal high colour, and a huge sense of frustration.

"Forty years we been married," said Ellie, "and he was forever busy at something. Couldn't stand to be closed up in the house…"

This being so, he only spent a day or two in miserable inactivity before he devised his own way out of the situation. Behind their neat house stood the low building where he kept his tools and made sauerkraut each fall; this was the refuge to which he now limped painfully each morning. At first he just sat and whittled his frustration away with his knife and any odd piece of wood he found under the bench; he was always a great whittler. But quite soon he began to whittle with a grander purpose in mind.

The leg healed slowly as his plan took shape. Back at work on the ferry, he waited impatiently for the day of his retirement — only a few months, thank God, and he would have his freedom and the time he needed.

Now he took to going back into the woods behind the house searching for something, and usually finding it: an odd-looking bit of dead-wood, a fallen branch, the glimpse of a particular bird. These he brought back to his building; and when he ran out of scrap-wood from the old boat-shop, he sent to the lumber-yard on the mainland for more, and he bought bird-books to verify his sightings.

Two or three years after the accident, when I called in on Ellie to ask if Herb was home, she would welcome me into her immaculate kitchen, offering a muffin just out of the oven and a cup of tea. The house was always fragrant with fresh baking, and Ellie was always as neat and clean as the house, a slim, bright-eyed woman. Then I would find Herb and his creatures, in the building.

He was at work at his bench, the floor around him deep in curly shavings; but he was also kindly welcoming to intruders.

From the raw wood gradually emerged a great array of birds. Some of them he painted carefully and correctly, following his books so that he could get everything just right. Others he varnished, leaving the grain and swirl of the wood to show through. There were finches, sparrows, swallows and swifts, sandpipers, terns, ducks of various sorts swimming (and one beautifully sleeping with his beak tucked into the feathers on his back), woodpeckers attacking tree-stumps, a flicker or two, an owl, hawks about to strike, necklaced loons...

Soon the shadowed shelves around the building were crammed with birds; it was time to expand. Herb placed his old sauerkraut barrels as trestles in the lean-to adjoining his workshop, laid sheets of plywood on top and gave himself a huge display table.

* * *

Parties of earnest bird-watchers descend on the Island from time to time, binoculars dangling from their necks, note-books in hand. All day they tramp through the woods, over the meadows, along the shoreline, until they meet on the wharf for the last ferry out. On the boat, they compare their findings, their voices raised in excitement as they relate some happy encounter. Sixty-six different sorts of birds they found on a recent trip, they said. Herb may not have them all in his shed, but it is still a sight to make the heaviest heart soar. If he were to open the window it would be no surprise to see them spread once-wooden wings and fly out in happy flocks, twittering, chirping, trilling, calling, hooting.

The air above us, then the land beneath our feet. Picasso had his "Blue Period," Herb had his "Turtle Period." As children, nearly seventy years ago, my brother and I kept pet tortoises, but I don't think I ever felt so friendly to any of them as I did to Herb's creatures: they melted your heart with their foolish faces on scrawny necks poking out from the heavy shells so variously and exactly marked. (Herb got a turtle book to put beside his bird books.) There were a couple of rows of them in due course, all ready to lumber off the table into the woods if opportunity presented.

Finally, from the sea around us, Herb conjured swimming things: a few disturbingly clever-looking sharks, a benign whale or two, a great halibut sliding gracefully through the water.

In due course, he began to sell them for a few dollars — retirement income. I had to limit my visits when our house began to resemble an aquarium in an aviary. It was impossible to go into the lean-to and come out empty-handed.

Hoping to further the growth of the fledgling business, while simultaneously and painlessly discharging part of my duty to our multitude of summer visitors, an area in which I was always remiss in M.D.'s eyes, I soon developed the habit of running these mainlanders over to the extraordinary workshop. Many left the Island with a bird or a beast, or, after Herb had acquired a lathe, a finely turned bowl. But he was no go-getting businessman; a child was likely to come away with a unique small bird for nothing, and when I brought a nun friend, he gave her a handsome bowl for the convent chapel. "I wouldn't ever take money from a church person," he said gruffly; but there was a smile on his broad weather-worn face. I doubt that he himself frequented either Island church or any other, but the life he led struck me as, in many ways, exemplary. His artistic temperament did not, of course, spare him the ordinary traumas of life. When Harry and Milly had both died, the will caused trouble amongst their children, and Herb and Ellie moved to the mainland to be near a kindly son. Wills, like property sales, can be bones of contention. I read one, more than a hundred years old, found in a forgotten drawer of our house, which left the west end of the kitchen to the widow, the east end to the wife of the oldest son. Even though the bereaved woman was to be supplied with twelve dollars a year, a bed and doubtless food from the land, medical attention when needed and a decent Christian burial, any housewife could guess that peace might be difficult to maintain between the "owners" on either side of that imaginary north-south boundary line across our small kitchen, even though both ends had a door to the garden, a route of escape. Neither, of course, had running water, nor any light beyond the sun, and, when it set, a flickering candle or an oil-lamp.

Those hands of Herb's, which gave so many gifts, were fitting ones for the heftiest, strongest man on the Island, huge, with fingers the size of young bananas. I always marvelled, watching them at work in their retirement, no longer hauling nets, haying, or tossing heavy freight around on the ferry deck, but gently, delicately sculpting wood. When, a couple of years after they left us, we went down the mainland shore to visit Herb and Ellie, her kitchen in the new house was as immaculate and smelt as good as the old one, and those grand hands were still at work in the workshop in the basement. It was brimming with new creations. I came home with an intricately branched piece of worn driftwood on which eight small birds are perched, ready to sing. They keep spring in mind during long winter nights. And on the living-room windowsill I always have the weird animal Herb whittled from an odd piece of wood years ago: it is unique in the universe, white with black spots, a long horizontal tail, large bat-like ears and an enigmatic grin on its blunt muzzle.

Chapter 8

Hearing

Man, on his way to Silence, stops to hear and see.
— Alice Meynell

An astonishing world has opened up for M.D. since we went to town and ordered hearing-aids for him. That was a year ago, and he is still adjusting to it. Things fade gradually, imperceptibly as one ages, and he is still getting used to the radical change; it is a shock suddenly to have one of the tired senses restored.

I am no longer the mysterious woman who appears with no warning footfall in the doorway of his study and waits until, with a start, he looks up from his desk. The cooking and the dishwashing no longer happen in a magical silence. Nowadays the plates clatter in the sink, the pots and pans bang against the stove-top, even chopping carrots produces a crisp little noise of its own. And there are other background sounds for which I am not responsible: the refrigerator hums, the wood crackles in the stove, a tap drips. It is a cacophony when you are not used to it, or to tuning it out.

There are also the voices — especially mine. It has been raised a notch or two each year for quite awhile, in order to reach him. Now it often comes to him as cross or impatient, although the words did not leave my lips freighted like that.

Sometimes M.D. turns the minute knobs in the hearing-aids and returns for a time to his previous peace.

I doubt that I shall have the dexterity or sense to do likewise should I live long enough to need such gadgets.

* * *

Once, long ago, I read a little treatise, "Du Mariage," by Balzac, whose own marital experience might be deemed curious. His message, as I remember it perhaps erroneously, was that the preservation of mystery was the essence of the thing. How horrified he would be by modern North America, where armies of experts make fortunes telling us ordinary people how to de-mystify everything from ourselves to the world around us and the heavens above us. I suppose I still remain a mystery to M.D., anyhow [...audible or not], and after all a modicum of mystery and uncertainty surely add spice to life.

Chapter 9

Roses

Oh, no man knows
Through what wild centuries
Roves back the rose.
— Walter de la Mare

One day I came up from the garden to find two splendid shining mackerel lying on the kitchen table, almost too beautiful to eat; but just what I needed for supper. Emily called while I was cooking them.

"Did you find 'em?"

"Yes, but I didn't know where they came from. I'm so grateful. How much are they?" I know that every dollar counts these days, with the fishery dying.

"Nothing, dear, nothing. Remember — you gave me a bunch of roses in the summer."

Fair barter, apparently, from Emily's point of view. A feast for the eyes is as good as a feast for the belly. Were she a mainlander, her clear sight would have been taken from her long since, her disordered life found to be in need of serious attention by social workers. Here, she finds compensations for her sorrows all around her; and no one tells her what she ought to do, least of all the men in her house.

* * *

The roses I grow and Emily loves are not the ones to be

found in florists' shops — each perfectly pointed bud on a long stem identical to its hybrid-tea sisters. Mine are the tough old roses which can cope with Island life like the rest of the inhabitants, and they have replaced most of the early perennials. The German and the Dane in the sunken garden are comparatively young; they saw their first summers in 1959 and 1965. But in the half-moon garden and placed haphazardly in the sod up the hill, wherever there was a pocket of good soil amongst the rocky outcroppings and the wild flowers, live roses from other countries and other centuries.

Watching me sceptically as I went about digging holes for the new bushes, William called out to me:

"When you goin' to stop? You'll be into the woods soon at this rate..." He was trying out his latest invention for smoking fish — not the usual smoke-house, but a huge smoke-barrel, lying on its side with a pipe from a peculiar sawdust-burning apparatus connected to one end. Today, years later, the old barrel lies abandoned in the tangled grass; and possibly William no longer thinks I am quite mad. In earlier days, he was unaware of Neighbour's well-tended flower beds, filled with life and colour and visible from every window in their house. His eyes were always on something else — the boat he was building, the sea — but the other day he brought her a bouquet of wild flowers, cow's parsley and muskmallow, which he had picked himself.

"Pretty, ain't they?" he asked, a little sheepishly, as Neighbour put them in a glass vase.

"The trouble is," he added ruefully, "when you begin to notice the flowers it means you'll soon be pushing them up. That's what they say, anyhow."

That may be true for the men; for the women, perhaps

it is the longing to see their flowers bloom once more which contributes to their longevity.

* * *

The old roses have tantalising names: I am teased by the thought that given the time I no longer have, it would be possible to discover the history behind each one. Amongst them are Cardinals and Kings, an Empress (Josephine, of course — she was a rose amateur herself, I think), a Sultana, countesses and captains, even politicians and explorers, starting with Jacques Cartier. It is often a temptation to plant a rose just because of her name and age, even though I suspect she may not flourish here. "Rose des Maures" is so ancient that her origins are shrouded in the Dark Ages; did she come with the conquering Arabs to Spain? And might she be happy near the "Austrian Copper," born in 1590, who flames here with burnished blooms each July? It would have been a joy to watch "Cuisse de Nymphe," some two hundred years old and politely named in English "Great Maiden's Blush." Then, there is the puzzle of "Nuits de Young"; who was this man and what was he doing with his Parisian nights that a rose should be named for *them?* And what was the "Tipsy Imperial Concubine" up to? Would she be friendly to my "Cornelia," the most innocent of creatures who flourishes so bravely just outside the south kitchen window? She asked for nothing grander than the small hole I dug for her through the surrounding shingle gravel, but must have sought and found her own nourishment far deeper down in order to grow to her present seven foot height. It became necessary to recruit M.D. to construct a simple wooden cage to support her multiplicity of supple branches clothed with dark glossy leaves and finally in early summer a cloud of small pink blooms whose fragrance on a breeze from the hill made my dishwashing indoors pleasurable.

There is no longer time to find the answers to all these questions, nor to plant more than a very few of the bushes I covet. From December to March, those I have sleep in the two rose gardens or climb the hill in twos and threes under a blanket of brush and snow. When I draw their coverlet back in early April they spring faithfully to life again. They are wives, lovers, daughters, as well as the great of this strange world, immortalised in the name of a flower; and also, of course, there is simple, perfect "Peace," elusive still everywhere on the globe except as a rose; she is indomitably ubiquitous in thousands of gardens in a dozen countries with her creamy pointed buds, opening so generously into wide blooms. They say she was smuggled out of Southern France to England for safety with other refugees, from under the noses of the Nazis, by her creator, the remarkable "Papa" Meilland, a man who married poetry with botany, art with science, and left us a unique legacy.

Names and labels can fool one, we all must painfully learn sooner or later, even if a dram of romance, whether political or anything else, for awhile helps down the draught of life. When I survey my glorious crowd in the gardens and up the hill each July, I realise that "City of Leeds" is as gracious, as dashing, as any of the lovely ladies, the aristocrats and adventurers, around her. She almost gives me hope that midland English cities, and all the others around the world, may not totally destroy their human inhabitants. "Leeds" is an ever-bloomer; once she has put out her first peach-tinted flowers in early July, she perseveres until a really lethal frost strikes. One year, after an unusually late and kindly fall, I cut a bouquet of her flowers for our Christmas dinner table. This is one of the few things I know to be veracious: a dated photograph of those flowers in a simple old vase on Jacob's pine table exists. It bears an astonished exclamation mark after the date; our northern island climate is seldom so gentle.

* * *

In the third summer of the sunken garden's flowering, Katie married. She is a tall girl with a lovely face — straight brows, straight nose, a gentle smile. She and her fisherman came over one July evening to ask if they might have their wedding photographs taken among the roses, and a week later, after the brief ceremony in the church, the whole wedding party trooped down the hill, the bride with the train of her gown hung gracefully over her arm.

We go in for grand weddings — and funerals — here. The brides wear white satin, the grooms rent sky-blue tuxedos; and the oak coffins are magnificent.

It was not always so, William told us when he kindly gave M.D. a half-dozen tinny coffin handles to use on storage-bins or some such. He had had them lying around for decades, since the times when you were buried in a pine box and there were no satin-clad brides.

On that sunny afternoon the photographer took dozens of shots of the young couple in all their finery, with and without the little flower-girls tripping over their long dresses, the small ring-bearer togged out in a velvet suit, the bridesmaids, and the two sets of parents, all with the roses round them. A little breeze played with the bride's veil, and everybody was smiling. Things had gone as they should.

"It's as good as being taken on the rose-lawn of the White

House in Washington," said Katie happily, as the wedding party trailed off to the Island hall for the feast. The teetotal minister who had married the couple would be present for the dinner but would leave discreetly before the wine flowed and the dancing began.

* * *

Hair-raising articles abound these days, no matter which periodical one picks up and leafs through, nor whether it comes from Europe, the United States, or Quebec. A curious one I came across recently gave me another dollop of food for thought about the lunacy of man. It described "Post-modern Gardens in France" during the 1920s and '30s. "Surreal" might have fitted their unnatural weirdness better. I never saw one, thank God… For Katie's sake and that of future Island brides, I'm glad that all I can manage is what the land and its lie demand and allow.

Happy footnote. Recently I heard that Monsieur Young was no post-Revolutionary gay blade. He was apparently a cleric; his nights were spent in mystical transports. The "Tipsy concubine," however, remains a mystery. Patience. Perhaps the tide will kindly wash in something about her one day.

Chapter 10

Flotsam and Jetsam

Ask yourself if you are happy and you cease to be so.
— J.S. Mill

Early on a diamond-bright New Year's Day, years ago, bitterly cold but blessedly still after a storm, we noticed through Jacob's tiny spying window a dozen trucks from back-along pelting over towards the South Cove. "Yes," said Neighbour when I called to find out what was going on, "they say there's good stuff over there and lots of it — came in yesterday."

We hitched the old trailer onto the even older (1954) army Jeep, grabbed a couple of Jacob's pitch forks and headed off after the back-alongers. Half the Island was there on the half-moon beach, gathering in the bounty; it was thick on the rocks and the sand, a feathery copper-coloured sea-weed. Red-cheeked parents, muffled up children with knitted toques pulled down to their eyebrows, everyone was forking up the stuff to spread on their gardens. Cheery words flew back and forth from group to group as they worked; it was a far cry from the Kelp Wars of earlier days, when our population was close to a thousand, and every inch of land was intensively cultivated if not being used for grazing animals or for wood-lots. A few loads of kelp or sea-grass could make all the difference to the next summer's yield of vegetables for some large family with a small garden. In those times men were down on the beaches with their pitchforks before dawn after a good storm, ready to garner the best fertilizer of all, kelp; despite their rubbery appearance, the long and frilly ribbons of the stuff rot down quickly on the ground. The harvesters were quite prepared to use their forks as lethal weapons against latecomers looking for easy pickings. That's what they say, anyhow.

There is little kelp these days and few of the lobster which love it and which were once so plentiful in the bay that they too served as fertilizer rather than as an expensive delicacy for the table; many vegetables enjoy lobster as much as humans do. And there are no more wars — of that sort anyhow.

There were other gifts from the sea, of course. Where the sunken garden now lies I found buried in the brambles a straight yellow cedar timber some twelve feet long and ten by ten inches square. Did that massive beam wash up here when some great schooner foundered in the bay? After a wreck, they say, it paid to watch the beaches, and even to take your boat out to the scene of the disaster and fish out floating debris. "You might hope not to catch a body by mistake," said old Harry sagely.

It was Charlie's misfortune which brought us the enormous turtle; it was hard on his nets but a winter's food for us. A little crowd of fishermen was gathering on the beach across the bay one September afternoon; joining them we saw what everyone was gaping at. Nobody had come across anything like it before, for the good reason that this creature was not meant to be in these waters. It was a giant leatherback, four and a half feet long, from warmer seas; somehow it had lost its way and, after what must have been a long and painful journey, ended up fatally entangled in the nets. The idea of eating its meat struck the men who helped Charlie cut it free as mad — even though Martin agreed that his mother had had no trouble in days gone by in stewing up a tasty dish from a gull or even a skinny heron, considerably less appetizing fare, it seemed to me.

This local anti-turtle prejudice benefitted us, anyhow. M.D. fetched suitable tools and sharp knives, buckets and bowls, and proceeded to dismember the creature, right there on the beach, slowly and carefully, with the natural interest of a pathologist in its curious structure. The men watched the operation with mixed feelings for a little while, but then drifted away shaking their heads. Plainly, we newcomers still harboured some strange and foreign ideas.

The turtle meat was lean, tasty and wholesome; we lived on it for months, braised, stewed, curried or made into a rich Victorian soup. And when the year of the turtle was over, the year of the halibut began and was equally beneficial to our health.

An urgent shout from Harv brought me running up from my gardening one afternoon:

"Hey! You people want some fish?"

There it lay in the back of his truck, fresh from the water, sleek and shining, a 100-lb. halibut. The sea had provided again. We spent half that golden summer evening sawing it up into steaks on the fish-board by the back door. It was so majestic a thing that knives alone, in our inexperienced hands, could scarcely have done the job.

Fertilizer, timbers, food, they all come in on the tide. And then, of course, there were the mainlanders.

* * *

"You know," said Edward with his shrewd blue-eyed look, "it's amazing what washes up here — especially the people." He is one of them, and so are we. Like us, he and Claire saw the Island once and came to stay, buying an old house on the other cove, even though they already owned a home in Quebec. But as he shouldered the scythe he had come over to borrow, I knew that the person he had in mind that day was the elderly Russian prince who had washed up right next door to us the previous week. From the open barn where Edward and I stood we could see him down on the beach, a slim and elegant silhouette as immobile as a heron, contemplating the rhythm of the small waves as they gathered just enough strength to break gently on the stones. He had landed up here by chance, but others have come by design, brought across the water by some flicker of hope that living on the Island will cure whatever ills beset them.

There are dozens of islands in our wider bay. Most of them are uninhabited except by cormorants and ospreys, gulls and seals, some are bare even of trees. This particular one was just a useful stopping-point for the first men who came here in their canoes. They found the fishing good around its shores and stayed for varying periods; in those days a hardwood forest grew on its five hundred acres — beech, birch, maple, oak and ash — and there was good water from springs and rivulets. A welcoming place to land on, and, for some, their last resting place. Up the hill on open land stands a clump of spruces, the tallest on the Island, which, they say, marks the Indian burial ground. No one cuts those trees.

The first European settlers arrived two hundred years ago: the Island was granted as a reward for services to the British crown to a couple of soldiers. They failed to fulfil their obligations and left, overcome by the hardships and isolation of island life. In due course, they were replaced by tougher folk from Germany, and it is mostly their descendants who still live here: they say that there was an old matriarch who ran things and that her blood runs in everybody's veins. After a funeral a few years ago I ran into Sadie walking, a little unsteadily after a nip to calm her nerves, up to the graveyard for the burial.

"Was Joe related to you?" I asked, a bit surprised to see her there. "I didn't notice you in the church…"

"Related?" she answered. "We're all one sow's litter here, you should know… I go up to the burials; but the funeral services put me off."

Not being part of the litter, I trudge up with Neighbour to the bare little church and sit at the back while the old hymns are belted out and the minister tries to stir the congregation with a sombre sermon, but I do not go to the graveside.

* * *

Edward and Claire, and one other travelled couple, have stayed — four people, and their visiting offspring, who have been accepted by now as real Islanders. Acceptance is something to be waited for patiently as we discovered. Sizing up intruders can be a lengthy process; people may cross the water with the best of intentions, but only close observation by our entire population will show whether they rate temporary visas or can be given immigrant status. Once that is granted, all is well from one perspective, but not necessarily from the other.

"If it weren't for hope, the heart would break," says Neighbour.

And, indeed, with high expectations and some flicker of that almost universal human longing for a place of refuge and escape lighting up their eyes, optimists pull up stakes and board the ferry. They are trying to avoid broken hearts.

Once out on the water, they jettison the baggage of half a lifetime and come ashore on what they take to be a small forgotten piece of Eden, saved by our wide and salty moat from the madness of the mainland.

"I've watched them over the years," says Neighbour. "They come — and then they go."

They do not realise that their baggage floated in with the merciless tide behind them.

* * *

When teaching jobs were plentiful, it was often hard to find a young person willing to take on our tiny isolated school, but a hopeful middle-aged woman leapt at the opportunity when she heard of the vacancy. Her husband was an alcoholic, and she snatched at the chance to work in a small paradise with no pubs, no liquor store. Our Island is various in its beauty: steep rocky cliffs to the south, woods to walk through, beaches in the two coves. A place of healing, she thought; and William was ready to rent them a good house he had inherited near the school. Hopes high, she signed the contract with the School Board.

She did not realise that the Islanders carry in their blood, together with a thousand extraordinary talents, the gene for alcoholism. The husband found plenty of men to drink with. After a year or two, the couple left; he died soon after. The plot of shore-front land on which they had planned to build their dream home ultimately went up for sale.

The American couple were weary of the horrors of urban life in the States. He had been a Medicaid doctor in city slums, she his nurse. It was depressing work. They sold up everything, bought an old cottage near Edward and Claire's place in the South Cove, had it fitted up with all sorts of modern conveniences, and moved in prepared to enjoy a peaceful early retirement. With them, they brought four frightening dogs the size of Shetland ponies — Akayas; the watching Islanders were relieved to see that these strange animals, as foreign as the great turtle had been, were kept fenced in on the property. Everybody loved the wife, a brave and gentle woman. She was lovely to look at still, and one could see why, in her youth, she had been able to make money modelling for a shampoo company. Her portrait, crowned with masses of auburn hair, had been splashed all over the continent for several years in full-colour advertisements. Now, decades later, and after half-a-dozen children, with all the vicissitudes entailed, she settled into Island life with ease and gratitude.

Her taciturn husband was the one whose baggage washed up on the shore behind them. He found it essential to keep in touch with the New York stock market, and, unable to communicate with the natives here, spent his time on the long-distance telephone playing it. When his games suddenly failed and it seemed he would have to go back to work, they sold the pretty house with its view over the South Cove and moved back to the States. Soon after that, they divorced; she, sweet woman, kept the dogs — which had, perhaps, been the only, and tenuous, link between their owners for years.

If certain ambitious would-be settlers arrive convinced after due thought that they have discovered the hidden resting-place of their dreams, others alight as nonchalantly as a passing gull. Some fifteen years ago, a high-powered civil servant, whose wife lived alone in Ontario while his children were scattered round Europe, took a quick look at the Island and was bewitched. He promptly bought an old back-along cottage, had it repaired enough to be habitable, and invested in a boat to go with it. Perhaps the man still dreams of the place: we haven't seen him for fourteen years, and the cape-islander has been rotting away on William's beach all that time.

Besides the steady stream of would-be permanents, who could supply a resident novelist, if we had such a thing, with plots and characters sufficient for a score of novels, there are others who arrive with the swallows and leave when they do, here for a mere fortifying taste or snippet of utopia.

Amongst this latter tribe was Art, who was one of the young people who had at different times adopted our family, usually because they lacked one of their own and ours was sufficiently numerous that we scarcely noticed one or two extras. When the Island adopted us, they were adopted, too — but only because, for some happy reason, they all seemed to know how to *work*. Perhaps this was because none of them had had an easy youth. Art had grown up in an orphanage, but had somehow picked up all sorts of carpentry and mechanical skills as he struggled, alone, to equip himself with two degrees. Whenever he had a few days of free time, he came down and helped M.D. scythe the hay, clean the well or put in kitchen cupboards. There was only one tiny dark cubby-hole in an eave for storage when we came here. The poor have no cupboards, Péguy pointed out; one might add that the skeletons the rich can hide away are in clear view here, which makes for a certain openness among us. Middle-aged now, Art works in the North, but he told us once he plans to retire to the Island and build himself a little house on the cliff-top. It left its mark on him; as he did on the watching Islanders. They will welcome him, the older folk who remember him, if they are still alive. They know he will bring no useless baggage with him, merely his own sensible interior universe, his clever hands and his willingness to learn.

The Prince was neither a would-be settler nor a brief summer visitor, and his advent among us was my fault. That summer I was, as usual, giving up smoking — a neatly concrete vice to overcome, as I frequently tell myself. So I was sitting up on the top deck of the ferry one afternoon rather consciously enjoying the glinting water, the idle small clouds above it, the distant hazy outline of the peninsula and wishing I had a cigarette between my lips to complete my contentment. In answer to my unspoken thought, two strangers on the bench beside me took cigarettes from their pockets and lit up. In abject weakness I asked them if I could "borrow" one — and so we began to talk. It appeared that the couple had just been thrown out of their pleasant holiday lodgings in Oldham and were in a state of some disarray. They had planned to be in these parts for some time, and had boarded the ferry to think things over, and maybe find another roof over their heads. Was there any accommodation available on the Island? they enquired hopefully.

"Well," I said, puffing slowly, thinking rapidly, "I know there's an empty cottage in the South Cove you might be able to rent. I'll run you over to look at it when we dock."

A second cigarette, during which I tried unsuccessfully to find out what was wrong with their Oldham lodgings — the truth only became apparent later — and we landed. A curious figure the man was as he stood on the wharf waiting for the Jeep, plainly a really foreign foreigner with his finely chiselled face and an air of distinction confirmed by the blue silk cravat at the throat of his well-cut shirt. His wife, plump and pleasant-faced, an ordinary foreigner, wore tourist jeans. I wondered how they had come together.

Our ancient vehicle had by then a plywood roof to keep off snow and rain, cleverly constructed by M.D. when the original canvas rotted, but no sides or doors, so passengers have an excellent view of our land — and sea-scape. It also has an immortal motor, as reliable today as it was forty-five years ago; and since we Islanders have been exonerated, by government fiat, from the necessity of licensing our wheels or our drivers, we do not fret about such things as blown mufflers, pathetically failing brakes, non-functioning headlights. After all, as Martin says, there's a Hand over the Island. He was describing how one of the lads, speeding around in the dark, had toppled his old car into the ditch and emerged unscathed from the wreck, whereas on the mainland he would for sure have been killed. "Happens all the time," Martin said and gave me a long list of should-have-been fatalities which could be explained in no other way. In any case, the Hand seems to work as well as a resident police force could, and is cheaper for the taxpayers.

My guests climbed aboard gamely, the man folding himself carefully into the back seat, where his knees nearly touched his chin, and the woman hanging on for dear life to the grab-bar opposite the front seat beside me. As we sailed up the dirt road past our driveway, I waved an idle hand at a cottage close to ours.

"Of course, that one's empty too," I called over my shoulder to the backseat. "The owner works in Montreal now."

As it turned out, that was the one the foreigners were able to rent, as well as the one they preferred because of its view over the water and its proximity to the post-office, which is, after all, still an important but not too intrusive link to the rest of the globe — and we must, of course, pick up our own mail.

Neighbour phoned the Montreal owner and arranged a satisfactory rent, William hooked up a water supply from his own well a little further up the hill, and the couple moved in three days later.

Dmitri and Melva added to the interest of that particular summer. I began to buy my own cigarettes again, naturally; but they made up for my fall from grace by giving us accomplished oil-paintings and curious snippets of hearsay history from elsewhere.

Melva, who was from the southern States, devoted her time to recording the details of island life. On our walls still hang a portrait of a freshly baked loaf of bread Neighbour brought her and one of an old earthenware jar she found in her cottage, in which she placed two of my roses. Dmitri would stalk over most mornings to "borrow" a few bits of wood for their old stove to take off the morning chill, and later in the day we would be invited to vodka and smoked salmon fillets ordered at great expense from the mainland — aristocratic tastes die hard — at their kitchen table.

Dmitri was a Dolgoruki. "A much older family than the Romanovs" he pointed out proudly. True, I thought, but did not say, if we only speak of recorded history: every Islander's antecedents go back as far as yours or mine. The couple were visiting in our cottage one afternoon, sipping scotch (we had no vodka) when he told us his life story. Melva, no doubt, knew it by heart; she was watching the fish-boats and the wheeling gulls in the bay through our tall living-room window and only put in a word or two during the last chapter.

Dmitri's father became involved in an assassination plot — was it in 1905? The liberal young conspirators gathered in some clandestine cellar to arrange the last details and assign the final roles one evening; but when he drew the black ball which designated him as the actual murderer, Dolgoruki grew faint at heart and left the meeting in silence. That night he fled to Germany.

Tormented by the knowledge of his cowardice, alone in Berlin, the young Prince immediately took the first step towards covering his traces and beginning a new life. Wandering down a narrow street, he noticed above a small grocery store the simple name Schmitt; he made it his own, and under it in due course he prospered, married and had children.

Dmitri, the oldest son, left Europe for North America at an early age, where he, in his turn, prospered and had a family but, now middle-aged, his Russian soul was not content — success had not satisfied him. One evening at a candle-lit dinner party in the deep South, his eyes met Melva's across the elegant table, and he knew what was missing. Rather soon, they both left their families and eloped to Majorca. There, in the mountains, they built a charming house and Melva painted. This idyllic life lasted only three or four years. Dmitri developed serious heart trouble, and in order to get good medical care for him the couple were obliged to sell their perfect island home and return to the United States. His health improved with first-class treatment, but they were left considerably poorer. When they became our summer neighbours they were taking an inexpensive holiday in these unfashionable parts. They had been kicked out of their simple but respectable lodgings in Oldham because the landlady frowned on their daily consumption of vodka.

Here we are more tolerant — we know what true alcoholism is. Sitting in their humble cottage or ours, Melva and Dmitri spoke and spoke, with nostalgia, of the warmer and more glorious Mediterranean island to which they had escaped brief years earlier when they had suddenly decided to disentangle themselves from North America.

We must be grateful for a few good memories to take into old age, if there is one waiting for us; and what that couple took from our northern island would be kindly at least, a small addendum to their first escape.

Neither Neighbour nor we heard what became of them after that summer faded and they left.

We are all flotsam and jetsam on the sea-shore of the world. Some of us wash up on kinder beaches than others; some of us are just more washed-up than others.

Chapter 11

Up in the Green Dell, Down on the Liar's Bench

> *If you want to know where you are going,*
> *Look at where you came from.*
> — African Proverb

Did the tiger, living up in the woods with our native wild cats, learn from them to become a bird-eater instead of a man-eater? Perhaps, looking from the cliff-top out to Hope Island one afternoon he noticed the great flocks of sea-birds which make it home and swam over to join them — and feed on them. In any case he ceased to slink into the house at night, and there were no more pug-marks on the path from the hill.

It was then that my ghosts took over the Dell; most came from distant places on the globe, but the translation to a tiny Atlantic Island seemed to please them.

The boy came first; he followed me up the gangplank from the Oldham wharf one summer morning. The wash from a passing boat shook the ferry for a moment and Grant called out in fear. He is only five, a curly headed sun-burnt child with a mischievous smile. He drowned a hundred years ago in a sudden squall which struck the small South Australian port where he lived with ten older brothers and sisters. His mother, who was my grandmother, had already

Up in the Green Dell

gone aboard with his eight-year-old sister to take tea with the Captain's wife in her elegant cabin on the great four-masted schooner moored to the wharf. A kind sailor had called to her as she went up the gang-plank; "I'll carry the lad up in a minute or two, Ma'am, and bring him to the cabin," and she went below. She was friendly with several of the women who regularly accompanied their husbands on the voyage to Port Pirie. Boats from all over the world traded there — inland, silver mines were being worked.

As the Captain's wife prepared to serve her guests, the schooner suddenly lurched against the wharf, then plunged away from it. There was a shout of "Man overboard!" and the sound of many running feet on the deck above. The gang-plank had parted and the sailor, with the child in his arms, was thrown into the churning water. The Captain himself dived in to rescue them. The sailor lived, but the child died; they brought his small body to his mother in the Captain's cabin and laid him in her lap.

I know the details of this death because my mother witnessed it; she was at the remembering age so the scene lived with her all her life. Many years later she described it vividly to her children. I never forgot it either. The tales we tell each other...

"Don't worry," I said to Grant, turning to take his hand, "this gangplank is strong." We reached the Island safely and Grant skipped along beside me as I made my usual tour of inspection of the gardens, the headland, the woods, the meadow, and finally, the Dell. In that peaceful green place he decided to stay. He looked around him with apparent pleasure, taking in the sea, visible but not too close, the shelter of the trees, the sun-dappled open space. Then he crouched down on his haunches and began building a small "house" of twigs and stones. "For little animals," he said, looking up happily, the sun on his curls. He had no hint of an Australian twang in his child's voice, any more than his grown brothers and sisters did. Their parents were early English emigrants, tinged with Welsh blood, and preserved their tongue intact as well as their aptitude for music. As the boy began busily roofing his neat structure with moss — child's play is always serious work — I left him to go down to the house to prepare for the two young grandchildren who were due to arrive the following day.

They were close to his age, but I doubt that they were aware that Grant sometimes came down from the Dell to watch them as they explored and played with the old fishing gear they found in the barn. A scientifically minded child, Michael spent happy days rigging up a system of ancient wooden "blocks" so that he could rope and haul enormously heavy things up onto the widow's walk. It was soon littered triumphantly with all sorts of nameless junk from the barn. I didn't mind this untidiness because that particular summer My Darling was remarkably cautious when out in his boat; there was no need for me to pace up and down on that little balcony, "spying" the horizon and wondering whether I should call on William and his lifeboat.

Elementary mechanics, a little nautical lore out on the water, a smattering of biology and botany — the children had a crowded, sun-drenched month. Helen six, made a sociological survey of the grandmothers on the Island and concluded that I was an inferior member of the species; unlike the other elderly women, I had refused to augment our grandchildren's meagre pocket money so that they could run over to the store and buy revolting-coloured candy or "pop" whenever the spirit moved them. Moreover, I refused to feel guilty when confronted by the wide-eyed child and her irrefutable statistics; but I was intrigued when Michael came home from the store one day with a poke containing two dozen rubber erasers.

"Do you expect to be rubbing things out for the rest of your life?" I enquired. "No, I'm going to sell them for 15¢ each when I go back to school — they only cost 5¢ apiece, and all my friends will want them at that bargain price" was the answer. Far-sighted even then, the boy had noted that there was a major sale in progress, and took what advantage of it he could with his couple of quarters. I did too, and sent the child back with a dollar to buy any bottles of that now rare liquid, ink, which might be going for a song. Rampant capitalism everywhere; but at least I was planning to use the ink, not sell it at a profit. It is more important to me than wine, and I don't know how to make it, although I tried to once, using iris petals.

Our very general store had supplied not only our own population but lighthouse keepers further off-shore with everything from fishing-gear and esoteric hardware to boots and marine paints for ages; now it had been sold to foreigners who knew nothing about such things, even though they were full of good will. They had bravely embarked on a new life as storekeepers in an attempt to escape the horrors of successful urban American careers. Sensibly, they decided to cut back on the extraordinary stock and deal only in staples, a small assortment of food-stuffs which would fit neatly on the shelves or in the ancient freezer, and, of course, soft drinks, chips and candies. There was a series of bargain sales on a variety of strange oddments.

The store survives, just, these days because the new owners supplement their income by running a bed and breakfast sideline, useful for occasional mainland visitors now that Beatrice no longer takes them in, and it still fills an essential role as a men's meeting place. A well-worn plank known as the Liar's Bench runs along the wall opposite the old counter, and it is nearly always occupied by three or four fellows with nothing more important to do for the moment than sit and reminisce, gossip or philosophise. The Liars (after all, one man's lie is another's truth and *vice versa*) are most of them too old to fish, the widowers, or those who are bored with their wife's company. Plenty of ancestral tales get told again on that hard seat, and rueful opinions are expressed about the way things seem to be going now with the sea and the world in general. Lately, Martin has been on that bench almost every time I have jeeped over for the milk which arrives here twice a week, now that we no longer have cows on the Island.

"How are you, Martin?"

"Bad as ever. Don't know what I'll be up to next."

Actually, he is well physically, pink-cheeked if white-haired after major heart surgery in the city recently, still chewing gum continually. By the time M.D. was able to persuade him to get treatment he resembled one of his own ghosts, ashen-faced, grey hair straggling down to his shoulders, unable to haul a net or even clean a fish. On the ward where he recovered he drove the nurses out of their minds with his irreverent language and behaviour. He had never previously been in a hospital, and God knows they are strange places, increasingly so these days. I hope his fellow patients were entertained by his haunting stories and bizarre wit; probably what he had to tell the other Liars on the bench was quite enough to make them stay away from hospitals. It was a difficult time for Martin, anyhow; shortly after he got home his vast barn and its eclectic contents somehow caught fire and went up in smoke. The Islanders took up a collection on his behalf, but his life had changed irrevocably; he did not try to rebuild it.

* * *

The store is now a mere cornerstore but it carries on one way or another, and as Michael flew off with his sister back to Ontario I surmised that he would, too. He had arrived with foresight and two suitcases, one of which was empty. This he filled carefully before leaving with a collection of Island treasures, including the sword of a swordfish, the tooth of an ox, a few dried star-fish, shells, chunks of rose quartz and fool's gold, half a pound of hundred-year-old square nails, the bag of erasers; the whale's bleached skull was too big to fit, but he would have popped in the powder-horn if I had not been watching. Finally, and most importantly, he packed the cardboard box containing a live snake. Probably it belonged to the family living permanently under the blanket of woolly thyme in the rockery, a small and pretty species, harmless to human beings, although I have seen them angry with each other. A couple were locked in a fierce but graceful battle on the gravel by the back door when I came up from the beach one July afternoon, rearing and striking at each other, forked tongues quivering, even drawing cold snake-blood. What were they fighting about? Certainly not the grand ideas over which modern men are prone to kill each other; more likely it was a matter of a lodging or a mate. And they did not kill, simply slithered away after two or three minutes, one to the east, one to the west. Michael's mother was not enchanted when his boxed snake survived the flight to Ontario and slid out alive; she shared with many of the Islanders a horror of the creatures, however harmless. Neighbour and I encourage them — they are an asset in the garden — but I have seen strong men here assault them with shovels and picks, a real horror in their eyes. Where does this terror come from? I suppose there may have been adders or vipers in the parts of northern Germany from which the first settlers came. We all cart our baggage round the world as we wander, whether we are plants, animals or humans.

The living children and all their paraphernalia consigned to the air, there was time to check up on the small Australian boy up in the peaceful Dell. Three paths lead there, one to the east past the old animal well which was shared long ago by Samuel's cattle and those of two other families, another cut by M.D. through the brush, dodging boulders and trees, but running fairly straight up the hill from the rockery, and the third, which I favour, along the cliff-top, looking out to Hope Island, the wider bay, the setting sun. After a couple of hundred yards this path rises steeply and runs perilously close to the edge of the high and crumbling cliff. Fifty or sixty years ago the massive headland rocks jutting out into the sea were dynamited and ferried across the bay bit by bit to provide ballast for the grand new government wharf, since when the waves have been nibbling away at the unprotected point. Fearing that visiting children might fall to their deaths if they ventured up that way, M.D. made a fine sign which he planted in the path where it became dangerous. "This Way Be Dragons," it read, "Turn Up Into The Woods." A seven year old American boy, whom we never saw before or since, came to the Island a week later with his mother; we were enjoying her company in the kitchen when the child burst in to demand a sword to fight the creatures.

That was a long time ago; I wonder what dragons that entertaining child is fighting now...

Doubtless my mother followed the dangerous path right up to the point when she came to join her brother in the Dell while I was occupied despatching her great-grandchildren. She always walked boldly wherever she was going. When I stepped out from green shadow into the sunny clearing the following day she was sitting on the mossy ledge of rock talking animatedly to the child looking up at the strong and lovely face I knew between the wars. Probably she was telling him some of the tales she used to read to us her children when we were Grant's age, no childish pap but the great myths of Greece, Rome, Egypt and the Norseland. Interesting. This was a word forever on her lips, lighting up her deep-set eyes. It might refer to almost anything: the taste of a new dish, ideas, current or out-of-date, characters in a book, unusual people or apparently ordinary ones she had come across, even to the colour of her five children's cheeks, too pale, too pink, too yellow perhaps, when we were sickening with some malady or other. Her world seemed to be endlessly intriguing. We youngsters used to talk, with our superior, sibling smiles, about the "bees in her bonnet"; but their buzzing meant an entertaining childhood for us.

One of her bees concerned the benefits of letter writing; her own experience kept that particular insect buzzing all her life. She had met Papa in Calcutta when she was visiting one of her many brothers, a friend of his who was also in the I.C.S. He, a lonely widower, much older than her and encumbered with a small daughter, had fallen unexpectedly in love and proposed. She was reluctant, having set her heart on pursuing a career and sailed back to her native Australia uncommitted. But over the ensuing months they corresponded every week, long reflective love letters, daily journals really, which took a couple of weeks at sea to reach their destination. She kept those he wrote; I have them now, but can only guess at her replies. In any case, in the end she was won over by the self-portrait he unwittingly painted with his words; and she always maintained that it had been an ideal courtship. Emotions due to proximity did not complicate the slow process of getting to know each other on a deeper level.

"Sir," said John Donne in a letter to Sir Henry Wotton, "more than kisses letters mingle souls." She would have agreed with him.

In 1911, Mamma sailed north from South Australia, Papa south from Calcutta, and they met and married in what was then a fairly peaceful and lovely island called Ceylon.

The unlikely couple agreed on fundamentals all their long life together, but disagreed cheerfully on everything else. Papa was appallingly punctual, Mamma hopelessly late for everything, aware that the best way to catch a train is to miss the previous one; he was tone-deaf, she was deeply musical; he was orderly, she untidy. Their children found this civilised diversity of views entertaining; probably it was educational too.

Once Papa had retired to England, shortly after the First World War, he always found time to make his letters remarkably brief; Mamma never lost the diffuse habit she had contracted during her courtship. Her long reflective letters flowed spontaneously all over the planet down through the decades to multifarious friends, relations, protégés, refugees; they were part of her hospitable openness, and always brought with them a breath of the southern English countryside. The last one she penned in her strong attractive hand reached me after her death. Half-blind by then, sadly unable to hear birdsong but still living, alone and self-sufficient, in the old house, she had walked firmly up the narrow village street, posted the letter, and dropped dead by the mail-box. The sudden death she had always prayed for.

Her other frequent prayer, she had told me when I had last walked with her in that wide Hampshire land, was for us children; not that we would pursue and find happiness, but that we would be courageous. No American dream for that Australian. Neighbour, I thought, whose best accolade for any friend of ours is, "She's a brave woman," would get on well with Mamma.

Papa had died less suddenly, in the same ancestral home; he had plenty of time to send a brief note first across the Atlantic. He hoped, he wrote succinctly, that Mamma would visit us on the one continent she had not seen, once he was buried. Obeying his wishes, and ours, before long she took a last boat across the ocean and then the splendid Trans-Canada train. This allowed her to become acquainted with yet more fellow-travellers; she loved the slow cocooned life on the old boats and trains which provided her with endless opportunities to make yet more unusual friends, and witness storms and sunsets at her leisure. Now she could enjoy the island which I had hoped she might live to see, its changeable waters and winds, relish what she would have called the "bracing" air.

Huge amounts of fresh air were essential to the family's health, one of Mamma's loudest bees always buzzed. Even when all the children had flitted, she went around the old village house every day after breakfast, flinging open the leaded casements whatever the weather. Papa, who considered that the ancient structure was sufficiently leaky without the addition of further draughts, would regularly follow in her steps ten minutes later, quietly closing every window. A couple of hours after that the double operation would, very civilly, be repeated, in silence. Now, in the Dell, winds might blow from any compass point, and there would be no chill in the air to bother Papa when he joined his wife.

Most of the people who came to the Dell, including the war-dead, brothers, cousins, friends, arrived when I was not looking and gave me a happy surprise when next I slipped up there, but Papa was very visible when he crossed the water. I watched him from the west window as he inspected the flourishing vegetable garden on the cliff-top, and then retraced his steps to take stock of the rose-gardens before following the middle path up the slope past the rockery. He had taken to gardening after his retirement to England from India in 1922, partly no doubt so that he could feed the numerous family cheaply (his pension was shrinking rapidly), but also, I suspect, because he found it a rewarding occupation. As soon as vegetables and fruits began to flow into the kitchen he applied himself to rose and flower beds, and a splendid rockery. He was still wearing his worn old gardening uniform, thread-bare plus-fours and gum boots, I noticed as he climbed the hill. He stopped now and again, apparently intrigued by the profusion of wild self-sown poppies along the way; they are different from any I have seen elsewhere in the world, a delicate mauve with fringed petals. Strangely, they seem to have their own sense of territoriality, never slip under the rail-fence onto Neighbour's land; but then, hers, all brilliant Flander's red, never trespass on my property. Both types are very circumspect

Island immigrants, which is more than can be said for the pheasants and some other taller living imports.

Inevitably, flocks of their friends dropped in on the parents up there under the trees; they were the grown-ups who appeared and disappeared in our childhood home, a steady stream of people who were forever talking about distant times and lands. Eavesdropping, we younger children picked up scraps of information on odd things — cobras and cholera, maharajahs and monsoons, pujas and plagues, suttee and Santal Parganis. The tales we heard gave us a jumbled sort of introduction to some recent history, that of our elders, and a little geography. We also got an inkling of the once solid meaning of the word "friendship." Since "support groups," like a lot of other efficient remedies for human sorrows, had not then been invented, people relied, for good or ill, on neighbours, faithful friends and, of course, widely extended family relationships, some of which naturally might be a nuisance as well as an asset, but must be accepted anyhow. When circumstances separated members of the wide circle to which all belonged, anyone who could hold a pen felt bound to maintain the links by writing letters to the absent. A strange habit, no doubt, from the point of view of their later descendants, who these days are taught in school by experts how to "communicate" in curious ways, but seldom how to write; from mine, however, it was an excellent custom, especially since it led to the invasion of the Hand Writers.

The ghosts from childhood had already been joined by my private ones, those known in the flesh in later youth. Anastasie in particular delighted Mamma there in the Dell. One summer afternoon of swiftly changing sun and showers I came upon the two of them on the path from the headland, deep in easy talk; there are no language barriers under those trees. "A very interesting and wise woman," Mamma would be thinking, and she would be right. Anastasie, who had grown up on a small hill farm in the Midi, was middle-aged when she befriended me in 1936.

She taught me more than she ever suspected about the world and its inhabitants; a silly girl of sixteen, I certainly needed a spot of good peasant education. She lives in my memory too for a less important reason; she was the only woman I ever met with hair longer than she was tall. She wore it in a huge round bun on top of her round little head, thus adding several inches to her tiny stature. One evening, when she came into my bedroom to say goodnight, she offered to demonstrate just what a crowning glory it was. The strong hairpins securing the bun pulled out, it fell around her and out onto the floor in a thin grey cloak. A strange little witch; except that no witch ever had so kindly crumpled a face. If she could not grow much of a skeleton, she certainly knew how to grow hair as well as how to think sensibly, as a farmer must.

Conscience called me back to work; I left the two women sitting on the rock slab under the pine. They were smiling, Mamma bending down to listen to Anastasie. Now the conversation had turned from the land and horses to hair: Mamma's had behaved oddly too, in a different manner. She had lost every bit of it in 1912, emerging from a nearly fatal encounter with typhoid fever totally bald. Her appearance must have given her husband of a year or so something of a shock, but he recovered; and so did her hair, although it never reached below her waist again.

As more and more visitors from the past crossed the water to join the democracy in the woods, it was more and more tempting to neglect the living ones. The latter could carry on with their stories on subsequent visits, I told myself, if I didn't spend much time with them on a particular one, whereas I might altogether miss some transient presence in the Dell if I stayed longer down by the water than was necessary to grow food for the hungry. The dead were so restfully self-sufficient, required no care at all...

Sometimes, when conscience failed to prick me hard enough, M.D. would ring the old school-bell from the back door-step to summon me back to present duty, and, hurrying down the hill, I would try to adjust my tenses. Time. It seems that even the all-knowing physicists are still having trouble defining it simply. The old and the very young always have, of course, and do not try, which may be one of the things which draws them together. The three-year-old and the seventy-three-year-old share a foreshortened view of the future, are more at home in the present; but the small child can live more simply in it, being unburdened by all those past tenses.

Periodically, Neighbour, almost despairing over some recent human folly detailed on the news, says to me as we sit briefly in her tidy kitchen or my untidy one, "Men must be the worst of all the animals." Looking around at the present with her, or looking back at the past up in the Dell, I can share her aching sorrow, her anger, over the problems in the world beyond the water and even over the small unnecessary ones on the Island, a silly altercation over boundaries, some lad's truck in the ditch, a Saturday night brawl. Fortunately, she and I have got into the habit over the years of moving on in search of some lighter angle on things, some cheering or ludicrous anecdote or other, so that we end up emptying our instant coffee mugs with shared laughter. "Did anyone tell you what the new minister said yesterday?" Neighbour might ask. (Plainly, he would be wise to think hard before he opens his mouth next…) Or: "Did you get the message on the T.V. about how to get rid of our wrinkles?" Even if she got a money-back guarantee on the stuff, I would hate to see Neighbour's face scoured free of life's etchings on it; but of course she wouldn't be such a fool as to try it.

We are two old women aware that the world is going to the dogs even more rapidly than usual now that a good many human beings have apparently evolved over the last two or three decades into creatures sufficiently advanced to find all their earthly contentment sitting alone gaping at a flickering screen of some sort, exercising merely a finger or two to tap a key now and again or flick a switch. Should they be smitten by a sudden sense of confusion or dismay when they occasionally leave their machinery, they can always take refuge in a health club or in the office of some therapist or other. Ignorant people like Neighbour and me have our exercise and therapy provided gratis by the land and water to which we are connected.

"What's so funny?" M.D. may ask as I come in smiling to heat the soup. It is both too complicated and too simple to explain. So I say, "I suppose Neighbour and I were counting our blessings."

There is a lot to be said for proverbs, wherever they come from. Pascal pointed out some three hundred years ago that all the good adages are already in the world; all that is necessary is to apply them. Not always easy even for those of us like Neighbour and me, who, though born half a world apart, were fed them almost with our mothers' milk; impossible for the young today who are reared on T.V. jingles.

Up in the Green Dell

In any case, we are not counting the chickens the experts and technocrats may try to hatch for the coming century with undue hope for the best. We know first-hand something about broody hens and their clutches, and hence that it is folly to make haste quickly. Even those benighted old Romans had twigged that much common sense. "*Festina lente*," they told their children, I seem to remember, wasting no plain words. But then, of course, one could choose to "strike while the iron's hot." Mixed messages, as usual, on an untidy planet which has always resisted simple answers.

The Hand Writers. They were bound to swell the population up the hill because they had long since introduced themselves when, for curious reasons and over several years, boxes and boxes of their letters and journals had landed on our doorstep. Very different hands had penned them over the course of more than two centuries, but they all lived on the fading pages: the Lowland Scots farming contingent, the Witch of Ning-Po, the young man who witnessed all the excitement in Paris during the Revolution of 1848, the maverick pioneering cleric for whom the icy wilderness of Northern Canada was home for forty years. Any correspondence from the feckless family scoundrels did not seem to have been preserved, which was a pity as it might have proved interesting; but what had reached us took up enough scarce time as it was. M.D. spent many winter months transcribing the Scottish letters, dating from 1762 to the Napoleonic Wars, on his machinery in the attic; he ended up with four volumes of them. Sorting through the boxes I often found myself sitting up half the night reading, under a steady electric light, dozens of others, penned by flickering candle- or lamp-light. The experience was almost as refreshing as if the hours had been spent in bed pleasantly dreaming, and more instructive.

Most of these phantoms were recognisable, but it was not until I eavesdropped on the conversation between the parents and the skinny little early Victorian woman that her identity became plain. Mary was not much taller than Anastasie and did not look like a witch either. Nevertheless, it was the title she had earned when, already middle-aged but at last free of family obligations, she sailed for China, just after the Opium Wars. Not an auspicious time for a foreigner to open a school, and especially one for women, there; but she had heard in her youth that Chinese women were oppressed by their men and denied an education, conceived the odd ambition to do something about this injustice, and set about mastering Mandarin in preparation for the undertaking. The general opinion in Ning-po was that this unwelcome foreigner was not only mad but menacing; she was accused of every sort of wickedness from kidnapping girls to cannibalism and witchcraft. Her school survived all the attacks as well as raids by bandits, and even prospered; it was still flourishing decades after its founder, ageing and in ill-health, had retired to Australia to die. She never saw England again.

The old cleric was familiar; I had met him almost in the flesh the May we sailed north up the bleakly beautiful Inside Passage to visit the youngest son still seeking his fortune in Dawson City. The boy and his father went off to Diamond-Tooth Gertie's gaming establishment one afternoon while I set out for the little museum. The giant of a man was standing just inside the door, glowering down from under bushy brows, mouth set in a hard line, beard long and white, surplice a little shabby — he never bothered with appearances. Was he thinking: "First it was those barbaric hordes of southern whites lusting after gold, now it's crowds of foolish tourists invading us as soon as the ice is out of the river?" (Reasonable sentiments. It was a mercy for our Islanders that the little gold mine in the South Cove had been swallowed by the sea before it could do them any harm.) The life-size Victorian photograph was daunting, but of course he could not know he was intimidating one of his few remaining close relatives. For forty years he snow-shoed, "tripped" beside a dog-sled or travelled long distances on the waterways between the mountains, at home with the wild and its peoples. In 1888, some ten years before the Gold Rush, he wrote: "There are few countries where a traveller needs less protection from man and beast than in the far North." He was speaking of his diocese, said to cover a million square miles, a vast "island" of snow and ice. Who else would be fool enough to revel in such an appointment? Shortly before the end he retired to the tiny, primitive log-cabin on the river bank, still known as the Bishop's Palace. Death caught him suddenly, sitting at his "desk," a couple of planks placed on boxes; they ferried the plain coffin a hundred yards downstream to the small Indian cemetery on the hillside. He is buried next to Skookum Jim, the fellow who made the momentous gold strike in what was then Rabbit Creek and soon became Bonanza Creek, just outside Dawson, almost a hundred years ago; he is the only white man there. What was he writing when his heart stopped in 1906? Yet another letter to his distant brothers, or a curt note informing the political or ecclesiastical powers-that-were about something that needed doing? During the Gold Rush he had not hesitated to demand that the government send the Mounties up to control the wicked white invaders. Or was it yet another book? Those old Hand Writers often produced books as well as endless letters.

Their publications formed an interesting small library. Some of the authors came from the same Dissenting Huguenot stock as the old cleric, who had himself dissented again to join the Established church, possibly because it had the means to shoot him off to some distant corner of the empire still bleeding red all over the map. The Bishop's theology may have been a little strange for an Anglican, even an extremely Low Church one, but his observations were acute as he wrote of Axemen and Auroras, Bears and Bowmen, Deer and Dogs, Fish and Flies, Jealousies, Moose and Mock Suns, Skins, Stars and Snowblindness, and set about translating the native languages. One of his more settled, but still Dissenting, brothers meanwhile set about proving that Shakespeare was Bacon, while also publishing material concerned with Natural History and Zoology. An earlier relative came up with an innovative book on the treatment of the insane, in 1804, every bit as entertaining — and unreliable — as many modern psychiatric texts. This fellow ran a successful asylum and had concluded from the study of his patients that the chief causes of lunacy were "love and religion." (Two hundred years on, should we add politics?) Apparently some of his therapy was remarkably effective, in particular an ingenious swinging, rotating chair he had invented, into which the sick person was strapped and whirled around. (William, I thought, our Island inventor, would be fascinated by the mechanism of this contraption.) Earlier still, well before 1800, the impoverished Lowland Scottish Laird struggling to keep his "quiver-full" of offspring in "porridge and plaiding" while looking after wide acres of farmland and the Solway Firth fishery (similar to the one we had here in the Bay of Fundy), found time to invent a new method of roofing farm buildings. The result was so strong "a man might dance upon it," he wrote. But he also found a moment or two to pen and publish, anonymously, a long book concerning the theory of music entitled modestly *An Essay on Tune*. Did he write it mentally as he jogged around about his daily work on horseback, saw to the planting of the great trees which still stand as a memorial to him? I confess that I fell in love with this man across the centuries; perhaps it was not surprising since he was M.D.'s several times great grandfather.

* * *

Another invasion kept me away from the woods for a week or more; an army of handsome Colorado beetles was attacking the potato plants. The experts in the United Kingdom, I had recently read, after decades of fighting it over there had finally banished the pest from their islands; now apparently it had taken refuge from persecution on our small acres. There was no mistaking the creature with his red-spotted coat and wickedness in mind. Assiduous attention to the garden was essential; for several days I applied myself diligently to it, only taking time out to look after household necessities. When I was over to the store that week for milk, Martin, on the Liars' Bench as usual, chewing gum, questioned me.

"You noticed somethin' strange goin' on around here lately?"

"Nothing out of the ordinary." It was doubtful he would be referring to garden pests; did he think I was looking somewhat haunted, not just old? For a moment I wondered whether I should invite him up to the Dell one day: perhaps he was still missing the company of his own phantom, was becoming bored with the talk of the other Liars? But I decided against such a rash step.

A few days later, the beetle apparently vanquished, I was free to take another look at my private democracy. Platoons of scarlet-jacketed British Soldiers stood to attention on either side of the shadowed path leading up from the headland; the patriotic old bishop would be pleased to know we still call this ubiquitous lichen by that name, I was thinking as I stepped into the sunlit clearing. But he was not there. Others were, however, the forerunners of the new wave of immigrants, those whose thoughts lived for me only on printed pages.

The two Emilys, Brontë and Dickinson, had arrived together and were standing under the pines, the huge dog Keeper sleeping at their feet. The women were already linked across time and an ocean, anyhow; they say that the Yorkshire poet's "Last Lines" were read over the New Englander's coffin because she had loved them:

> *No coward soul is mine,*
> *No trembler in the world's storm-troubled sphere*

Three would-be poets amongst the war-dead joined them as I watched. The dog did not stir. Would one or two more kindly animals put in an appearance? It would be pleasant to see Mealy again, the gentle cow I used to milk now and then as a child.

It was no ruminant who turned up the following week but another man, as tall as the old cleric but at least twice as heavy, the weightiest democrat of them all, G.K. Chesterton; yet if he was a patently human immigrant, one might say that he did know how to ruminate to some purpose, aloud as well as when going about his humble journalistic work or writing a book or two on the side, tossing off a poem or a picture. His mere presence caused gales of ghostly laughter amongst the Dell dwellers, including the dozen or so children who were now Grant's playmates. (Three of them were native Islanders, one a native Indian orphan, Owinda, adopted by the Bishop's wife, another a ten-year-old German Jewish boy who had haunted me since the August of 1938. Too long a story to tell, but it had ended with the child carefully hanging himself on his family's farm near the town I was visiting that summer, Heidelberg; if he were dead, the child had understood, his parents might be able to escape from Germany.)

Chesterton's laugh was as much a part of him as his huge girth; there was no hint of a superior snicker in it, whether he was in congenial company with a gang of children, drinking in a Fleet Street pub or a village one, or debating serious issues in a public forum with the intellectual luminaries of his day, nearly all of whom disagreed strenuously with his peculiar views but loved the man with the irrepressible laugh who held them. "A towering genius," G.B. Shaw called him. There was clay in the feet which supported the tower; but I was told by the person who knew him and his wife best, the woman who was for years his secretary, almost their daughter, that the admixture was insufficient to threaten his vertical stance. That virtual encounter with G.K.C. in 1943 I owe to Adolf Hitler. He was dropping bombs that summer on London; I was ordered to leave the hospitals there for the many wounded and get out to the country, where I would not be such an unnecessary nuisance, to have the baby who was due. The stranger who took me in in G.K.C.'s Buckinghamshire village was Dorothy Collins, by then his literary executor. She offered such interesting hospitality that I was reluctant to go to the local Nursing Home to give birth to our only daughter; I managed to delay her advent for two and a half weeks.

Friends of many varieties Chesterton could make without any effort as he lumbered on through the first thirty-six years of this century; enemies were a different matter, very thin on the ground. One or two press barons considered his Distributist opinions, and, no doubt, his humour, so dangerously subversive that they tried to nip his journalistic career in the bud by forbidding the very mention of his name in the pages of their papers. This ploy did not work; the laughter and the clarity of vision that came with it won out over them as well as over the earnest propaganda of his argumentative friends.

A crowd of the latter were bound to turn up soon, and would naturally include H.G.Wells and G.B. Shaw; and they would be accompanied by some less disputatious people: the village policeman from Beaconsfield, a flock of children, a poet or two with his old friend Walter de la Mare, the original Father Brown, some fellow journalists, E.C. Bentley, who invented "clerihews."

It was a lively summer under the trees; many of the new wave immigrants hung around until G.K. disappeared as the last of the dandelion seeds parachuted off in the breeze. They were his favourite flowers; and like them his ideas and aphorisms continue to crop up in unlikely places, even as far afield as Japan. Time has proved them to be more prescient than those of his remarkable adversaries. We can't choose the period we must live in, but we don't have to succumb to it, nor espouse ephemeral gospels, whatever our current masters tell us. We are still free to plagiarise the past, kidnap anything worthwhile we may come across there; we may die of inanition if we don't, or choke to death on some fashionably deconstructed bone.

"So what is this thing, Distributism?" a visitor at my kitchen table that amusing summer wanted to know; she had heard of every -ism except that one. I could not give the questioner a satisfactory answer, of course, since G.K.C. wisely never attempted to put the ideas behind it into the fatal strait-jacket of a party platform; there were no crowd-rousing slogans, no magnificent manifestoes. It is nevertheless an -ism which would provide a bulwark against rampant imperialism, corporate pan-capitalism, consuming materialism, lunatic utopianisms of one type or another — were it to be generally adopted. My guest relaxed when I assured her this was unlikely to happen. The essence of it may be a forgotten commodity called common sense, married to a proper understanding of "the crooked timber of humanity," something which is resistant to being neatly straightened out, whether by magic or medicine, politics or preaching, or any nostrum so far invented

Another of my literary icons, the little possum, Pogo, saw eye-to-eye with the massive G.K.C. on the subject of humanity. "I have met the enemy," said Pogo to his fellow swamp-dwellers sometime around 1960, "and he is us." A good deal earlier G.K. had published a book with the title "What's Wrong with the World?" When someone asked, "Well, what is?" He answered cheerfully, "I am."

Down on the cliff-top vegetable garden that summer, if the wind was right, faint echoes of the laughter accompanying all the talk up the hill could be heard; but I had to leave my weeding and walk up there to check on who had newly joined the company. One week it was two explorers, Gertrude Bell and Freya Stark, and then the enigmatic Russian concierge from pre-war Paris days, the insect man Fabre and a few later scientific types such as Piet Hein and Loren Eisely, the odd novelist, artist, musician... It was a crowd all right but a uniquely agreeable one. Once, decades ago, in Nazidom, I watched a group of ordinary young people, spell-bound by a demagogue, metamorphose suddenly into a mindless predatory mob. The horror of the experience cured me of crowds for life; it was one of the attractions of becoming an Islander that here it would be impossible to muster a crowd, however hard some interloper might try.

* * *

M.D. benefitted to some extent from all the comings and goings in the Dell when I took to serving him something besides our usual Island fare. Suddenly remembered dishes appeared from time to time: cassoulet for Anastasie, paprika chicken when several Hungarians turned up, borscht for a few Russians, couscous for an Algerian or two, and of course curries of one sort or another, plus dahl, in honour of Tagore and Gandhi and others from the sub-continent. M.D. wondered what had come over me; was I belatedly becoming a devoted cook? This was unlikely; the tolerant man knew how comforting I had always found the profound poem about food written long ago by one of the visitors up the hill, Walter de la Mare. By substituting "M.D." for the original subject of the verse, a "Miss T.," I could both preserve the rhyme and avoid fussing over the stove, especially if I also mentally italicised the word "whatever." Then it read:

Up in the Green Dell

It's a very odd thing —
As odd as can be —
That whatever *M.D. eats*
Turns into M.D.

He has done very well on "whatever" since the day we were married decades ago. Anyhow, the sudden variety in our meals was a passing phase; and, out of wifely charity, I did not, in memory of Mamma, begin to cook our fish according to her unpalatable recipe. She had a mania for oversteamed bony herring and old cod: not only cheap, but, said the health gurus of the day, good for our brains. Now they swear it is good for the heart. Experts were not infallible then, nor are they now. In any case, that was a happy summer, both down by the water and up in the woods. Democracy, someone said (probably Rousseau) is a system for gods, unsuitable for mere mortals; it certainly worked very well for the dead, even if it was impossible to guess how such a disparate electorate might vote if given the chance.

Chapter 12

High Summer

The heartbreak at the heart of things
—Wilfred Gibson (Lament)

Through all the long days, beginning in late April, Neighbour and I meet less in our kitchens than over the rail fence which William put up between our two properties some years ago when his gnawing grievances over old Samuel's wickedly devious land plan of 1920, based on a much older one, and properly registered though it might be, erupted for the last time. It became essential for us, the perfectly legal inheritors of the twenty-five acres of the house-lot, to settle as best we could the mysterious, to us, question of ancestral ownership. A surveyor was brought over, a sober one this time, there was much trudging around, measuring, shouting back and forth; but in the end William was satisfied and a new deed was signed, granting William his coveted strip of our land. Martin turned up a couple of days later to report that half the Islanders were saying we had been diddled by this agreement. "You been wool-pulled," he told us, "that's for sure," and shook his head incredulously when we said we weren't all that concerned, peace between neighbours being more important than a bit of beach.

Leaning on the controversial fence, I watch Neighbour's small deft movements with her ancient hand-made hoe —

like all the tools we inherited from Jacob and indeed his father, Samuel, it is far more efficient for our purposes than any modern gadgetry. She senses my presence and grateful for a small break joins me. "How did the roses come through the hard winter?" she wonders and, "Are your beans up yet?" Looking over her shoulder I see hers, neatly curled to ease their passage to the light, are breaking through the crust of the soil. It is harder for them on her stony patch of land than for mine in the softer deeper earth on the cliff-top, but we grow the same beans bearing the excellent name "Provider"; they never fail to live up to it. Neighbour's potatoes are up too of course, but they are planted in the garden behind her house with the brassicas and are meant to be in William's domain, although as time slips away he bothers less and less with it. From year to year, the Islanders save seed from their crops; why waste good money in a seed-store when the garden gives you all you need? Each fall, I keep half a bucketful of Esther's Early potatoes to cut and plant as soon as the frost is out of the ground, ever since chatty Pat's old mother came over that first gardening spring with a basketful and demonstrated the best way to plant them. She was a small dumpling of a woman — still is, although now she rocks in a chair all day in the Old People's Home in Oldham, her body ever rounder, her wits quite gone. Her method was simple: bending double rhythmically from her hip-joints like some mechanical wooden toy-soldier, she whisked out a deep hole in the earth with a long narrow trowel before popping in the morsel of living potato flesh and covering it. Thence forward I never lacked early potatoes to grow alongside a few rows of Yukon Gold or some purple main crop keepers; but I prefer to plant kneeling than bent in two, even though I still am gratefully able to touch my toes.

Esther lived some hundred years ago, long before the ferry linked us to the mainland; to make a spot of cash, she had her man sail her to Oldham with a boat-full of sacks of potatoes to sell to the wealthy New Englanders who had built grand summer homes on the long and lovely arms round the Oldham harbour. One kind lady from Maine advised her she would do better if she could supply an earlier variety, and promised to bring her some seed the following year. She did, and the descendants of those potatoes are still the first things we put in our gardens each year. No doubt they were born with a much grander name, but Esther's Early is good enough for me. They are modest plants above the ground, but below it prolific. Summer is at its best when we dig the first delectable tubers and eat them the same day, cooked with young mint leaves, sprinkled with the flourishing parsley. I suppose that all these Island years have preserved our taste-buds from the excesses and artificial refinements of city eating; we still relish simple fare, and our happy palates still mean we are satisfied with cheap living.

When half the Esther's Early have been eaten, it is time to look to the hill for the wild harvest of berries — tiny strawberries, fat raspberries, gooseberries, blueberries, growing wherever on the rough slope they have chosen to put down brave roots. Once established, they struggle mightily to take over the network of narrow paths we have cut laboriously through the brush and the woods over the years. At one time or another, I grew them all, tamed siblings of each, in the garden. Now, like me, the garden is shrinking and I am content to leave some of the work to unaided nature — the fruit is smaller than mine was but no less tasty; only the red and white currants do not know how to look after themselves.

Infant potatoes, spinach and lettuce, berries: it is time for the yearly flood of fair-weather visitors to wash over us. They will come alone or in groups, sometimes even sail into the bay and drop anchor off William's rickety wharf. Most come for a day, some for a night or several; the house comfortably accommodates six or seven in the attic rooms, and if there is an overflow of children they take sleeping bags out to one of the barns.

The need to size up the wishes and appetites of all these disparate people drove me to invent, for purely selfish reasons, a soup-kitchen system which I dignify with the name of Island Hospitality. It is a philosophy which has operated smoothly now for more than two decades, allowing me to pursue my pressing work with no more than an extra daily half-hour spent in the kitchen while granting untrammelled freedom to the flocks of visitors who begin to appear soon after the swallows. M.D., the most conscientious of men, very seriously questions every year whether I am fulfilling my duties as a hostess, quite unaware, because his gardening has always been restricted to the charitable business of scientifically producing huge mounds of compost for my use, that there is an even sterner voice calling to me from the land. I pay scant attention to his remonstrances to my minimalist attitude, fortified by chance remarks from departing guests and latterly having witnessed the star performance, from my prejudiced viewpoint, of the courtly old professor from Europe who once turned up with a group of younger people. After the standard Island lunch, chowder if one of the fishermen has been over with a fish or two, otherwise, garden soup, any salad that is up, berries when ripe, eaten off the long table on the lawn made durably of two-by-twos years ago and now shaded by the mathematically perfect, but still romantic, "band-stand" cleverly constructed over it by M.D., the charming man announced with a smile as he finished his glass of dandelion wine:

"And now, my dear, I feel sleepy." Not the easy confession he would have made after dining out in town. He might be surprised to learn that I count him as an invisible ally in my anarchist battles against certain constrictions, whether those that are now politically or socially correct or those that were in my youth, and his. When he sails over again, I'll talk to him more before he falls asleep.

"A deck-chair or a bed?" I asked. He chose the brass bed in the attic and slept in the heady sea air blowing through the open window while his somewhat younger wife tramped off with the other guests to gather baskets of the exotic chanterelle mushrooms which grow in abundance under the spruces on the headland; they say these orange fungi cost a fortune on the mainland. I enjoy them chiefly for the way they glow like tongues of flame so unexpectedly in the green shade.

Some who come, often from distant places and continents, are old friends or even relatives we knew in earlier chapters of our lives; for the more local mainlanders, who turn up as regularly as the humming birds, the idea of a brief Island escape is what brings them. But occasionally the dark shadow behind the taste of liberty obscures the promised hope. An English woman arrived one July with a small daughter; the child delighted in the beach, the woods, Neighbour's kitchen, but the mother became distraught within a few hours. Dressed for the whole week in what she called a cow-gown — a long loose garment which disguised her over-buxom figure — she spent hours pacing up

High Summer

and down the widow's walk looking out over the bay, not with pleasure but with fury. "How can you stand it?" she wanted to know. "All that bloody water everywhere you look…" For her, a woman divorced both from a certain man and from the world around her, our innocent little island was Devil's Island, a moated prison. Only the lively child was sad when the ferry carried them back to the din of civilisation.

Less dramatic than the hand-wringing performance of the Lady Macbeth on the balcony but just as deep are the practical concerns about being cut off from the familiar props which the brief voyage from Oldham seems to produce in a number of day visitors. One spoke for several as we sat in the "band-stand" on an afternoon of brilliant sun. A sudden warm wind had blown up and white-caps were dancing over the water; they would only die when the west flamed and the wind fell asleep. Perhaps they were boisterous enough to disturb my old friend's sense of peace; she was a Quaker, so knew all about peace, but a nobly active one.

"I suppose it's all right to stay on here in this isolation," she said, "if you don't mind dying so far from help." No doubt living here herself she would miss not only some sense of civilised safety — doctors and hospitals on tap, police and fire departments on hand — but also a wide theatre for the many activities she pursues still for the betterment of the world.

When it comes to death, I feel closest to Neighbour, who often tells me, "Don't weep for me, Rachel, when I drop dead." Like her, I would rather die alone on the beach or in the moonlight silver on my Island bed than in a wailing ambulance or hooked up to bizarre machines in some noisy hospital ward. A matter of temperament, I suppose;

A Treasured Island

or is there an Island view of the greater world which casts us in the role of interested but quizzical spectators rather than participants in the ceaseless drama unfolding beyond the water? In any case, neither Neighbour nor I is likely to have much choice in how we die; but we will not weep for each other, merely be grateful we met.

Sometimes, talking with Neighbour or Lucy, still living alone in her well-ordered body, now over ninety, in her equally old and well-kept house overlooking the bay, or listening to Ethel explain how she and Pete jointly make great barrels of sauerkraut each fall and satisfactorily divide up the house and garden work, I feel that I am living in a last peasant outpost of sanity in a mad world. In dealing with the aggravations and disasters which confront them, few of these women rush to the mainland seeking advice from the pullulating certified experts standing ready to dispense the latest notions on the pursuit of happiness. Counselling and marketing are the twin growth industries in these odd times, and much of the world seems happy to accept them also as the twin authorities to which the hoi polloi should humbly bow. Insulated by those kind miles of water, the older folk here are still conscious that good sense is as necessary as good will to survival; they have had to keep their eyes and ears open since they were toddlers and have long since become their own authorities on human and the wider nature, whether in their boats, on their patches of land or in their homes. I doubt that in applying their unaided native wit to the ecology of the Island and their own daily lives they have made any more grievous errors than that army of certificated missionaries in their mainland bases.

I heard through, I think, Oliver Sacks, that there is a southern island on which all the natives are born deaf but are content with their condition. Some expert will, no doubt, one day want to cure them, make them "normal," just as some ardent animal lovers wanted to rescue the sheep who used to flourish on a small island within rowing distance of the South Cove. They lived there year round, regularly supplying splendid wool for our women to spin and weave, until the R.S.P.C.A. heard about them and ordered that they be brought back to the main island and cared for "properly." The foolish animals knew how to survive on Sheep Island, but soon sickened and died on the crowded mother island. Decades later, ironically, that tiny island was bought by a vagrant group of ex-hippies seeking a summer refuge; they were less adaptable than the sheep to those bleak surroundings and could not have lasted long, year round.

"Don't meddle with the land," we were advised once, in a different context, by Lester's father-in-law, and perforce took note of what he said. One might add, although few educated experts would agree, "Watch how you meddle with the vegetable, the animal and above all, the human." Perhaps only some of us were meant to live on islands, always subject to the implacable power of the sea, our private remedy for hubris. Despite all the happy pronouncements of the knowing classes elsewhere, here we know that there are no quick fixes for the human condition. I suppose it is our mutual acceptance of this simple truth which enables Neighbour and me to understand each other. Her sorrows have not been mine but we have each lived through our own allotted ones somehow, and when I watch her and Ethel's pure pleasure in some random flower or bird or even rock (Ethel in particular appreciates "handsome rocks"), a childhood recollection of Blake rises in my old memory:

A Treasured Island

Man was made for joy and woe...
And when this we rightly know
Through the world we safely go.

Safely? Only those fortunate ones among us who survived the wars and wickedness of this progressive century. If we did, it is right that we should take note of the joy. No experts are needed here to teach the Islanders a constant sense of pleased surprise in their surroundings; nor that, in face of the inevitable adversities, courage is necessary. And that, in the last resort, we are our sisters' keepers.

* * *

There is, however, one expert we gladly welcome every year, the Weed-Lady. Sometimes she comes as part of her job — she has some respectable position in the Department of Agriculture we understand — sometimes just for pleasure, bringing her old mother with her and staying for a few days at Marian and Desmond's bed-and-breakfast house beside the store. She is in her late fifties, a tranquil woman with iron-grey hair in an untidy bun, an elegant face finely lined from exposure to the elements, and well-used hands. Her arrival is cause for jubilation even among the twenty children in our school since she first quietly instructs them in their classroom about the remarkable Island flora and then leads the chattering excited pack up past our gardens on a natural treasure hunt into the meadow and woods. The women too benefit from her admirable familiarity with everything that grows in this corner of the globe; it is an intimacy, not some theoretical expertise, she shares with us.

Some time ago, a plant we had never seen before turned up on the land. Was it washed in on an evil tide or dropped by a passing bird? We do not know, but once in the soil, it seemed to be invincible despite the delicate look which made one think it was merely a maverick cousin of the pretty portulaca which flourishes each summer in the rockery. No matter how hard and frequently we hoed and weeded, it persevered with amazing speed in spreading itself in a thick mat of charming star-shaped leaves apparently designed to choke and kill flowers and vegetables. We gardeners were desperate.

"Ah," said the Weed-Lady with her slightly accented voice and pleasant smile, "you just encourage it by attacking it, you see. The fiercer you are, the fiercer it is. There is only one way to manage it. Since the smallest thread of a root or the tiniest piece of a leaf will start a new plant, you must carefully pull each little one up by the root and *burn* it." Neighbour and I got down on our knees carefully obeying her instructions, gathered buckets full of the witch-weed and rejoiced as we watched it converted into smoke and ashes. "Root it out" says the Bible; we did and have scarcely seen it on our land since. It goes by the deceptively pretty name of purslane, I think.

* * *

Recently, I noticed the Weed-Lady waiting on the wharf, half-smiling, imperturbable in the midst of the bustle and shouts as the high-school children disembarked from their sea-going bus and the freight was unloaded. "I would trust that woman's wisdom far beyond questions of nefarious plants," I thought. And as the boat turned and set off again for Oldham I caught a happy glimpse of her standing alone on the upper deck unashamedly smoking a weed we both enjoy.

Limping back home in the old Jeep I began to wonder why so very few people inspire trust, in me anyhow. The little gallery in whom I preserve real confidence, whether I always agree with them or not, whether they are dead or alive, whether I know them only from memory or the printed page or in the flesh, is entertainingly diverse. G.K. Chesterton indicated once that no soul can put another under a scientific microscope; and then I remember George Orwell, who retreated to a much wilder island than ours to write his last and prescient book, *1984*. Perhaps he did not believe in the "soul"; but he had a habit of using, and meaning, words from an age that did — "decency," "responsibility..." The degradation of our language since his death into ephemeral jargon has probably made them, with a thousand others, obsolete. Neighbour has no difficulty in agreeing with me that we now live in an Alice in Wonderland world in which words from the mainland merely mean whatever the speaker for the moment wishes them to mean.

Perhaps, I thought sadly, rounding the bay, the most useful thing I ever did to fulfil my duty to the rest of mankind was to throw myself into the role of Alice in a school play nearly seven decades ago. I was nine at the time, and it was a painful business; my hair had to be scraped back from my forehead to match the Tenniel pictures of the bewildered child, and my older sister was an embarrassing Red Queen. But despite the footlights illuminating our performance, I doubt that many people left the little theatre deeply thoughtful about the human condition.

Orwell died in 1950, Lewis Carroll and Lord Acton long before. Such people were always lonely, confined in one way or another, to a small island.

"I never had any contemporaries," said old Acton towards the end of his life. As I bumped over the last potholes in the shore road, his ghost whispered in my ear, "Nearly all great men are bad men," and then, of course, "Power corrupts and absolute power corrupts absolutely." The Jeep coughed several times as it tackled the little hill to our driveway, and I remembered the Oxford wag who quipped, "Yes, power corrupts, and horse-power corrupts absolutely." Our Island horse-power is frail; for so long we were used to ox-power. I hoped for a moment, as I parked the ancient vehicle — no hand-brake to bother with — that it was uncorrupting. The trellis beside me was covered by the exuberant clematis starred with white and royal purple flowers. "Bees Jubilee" it is named. There were clouds of them humming round the blooms.

* * *

During the long winter nights each year I dream vividly and often of the high summer to come — the faithful return of the swallows and hummingbirds, the faithful new growth of food and flowers, birch and spruce, juniper and bracken. But just as inevitable as the happy fulfilment of these dreams are the moments of dark horror which shatter us suddenly and fill us with the knowledge of our own smallness, our final impotence. The fertile peace and brightness round us become an insult to our feelings; surely midwinter should be the time of sorrow?

Experience has taught me to be suspicious of too blue an August sky, too fragrant a gentle breeze. Is this dangerous weather, a corner of my mind asks. An adjacent corner, the historical one, sees me, a young woman, standing in an English garden, equally as fragrant as this summer one in its own way, in, probably, 1944. (That corner of my mind is thoroughly incompetent with dates after the birth of Milton in 1608, for some reason; I do not bother the poor thing with modern history.) I have a very small child by each hand, and looking up into a clear sky I see a "buzz-bomb" approaching. It has ceased "buzzing," sails silently on, which means that at any moment it will fall and kill everyone within reach. I stand there in the sunlight, frozen in anticipation, my grip on the toddlers' hands tightening. We lived, but three miles away a dozen other mothers and children died.

Some summers ago, I got up off my knees after pulling weeds around the roses for an hour and looked across the bay. It was empty, serene, one loon meditating on the water close to shore. But further out was a boat behaving strangely, circling round and round in a lunatic fashion. Was the rudder stuck? Where was her owner? She appeared to be out there on her own — there was no sign of a captain.

It was not the rudder but the sailor who had given up. He had borrowed the boat from a fisherman, boarded her with a pistol in his jeans' pocket, and shot himself in the head when he was out on the water. The distraught boy was only remotely an Islander, had merely spent a penniless and tumultuous young summer visiting the place in which his grandmother had lived and died.

He had made the mistake of falling drastically in love with one of the Island girls, who had other plans for her future.

As I watched, a couple of fishermen left the wharf to see what was going on; nothing goes "unspied" round the bay. They brought the circling boat and the wounded lad back to shore. He lived for three days after he was taken to a mainland hospital. The girl took longer to get over the situation she had provoked merely by being her quite simple self.

High Summer

A year later, sorrow came closer. I was weeding again, this time down a row of spinach, a rest after the painful triage of two rows of carrots. As the omnipotent (bar the power of the elements) gardener, I must decide each early July which feathery little carrot plant should allow its siblings to flourish by dying itself. Eugenics. And when an expert on humans rather than vegetables decides which specimen should live, which be thrown on the compost heap, how many mad Newtons, Beethovens, Einsteins will we lose? Even Darwin wrote in a letter to a relative once, hearsay tells me, that their own family was so infirm that they should probably cease propagating their faulty genes.

Perhaps because I was no longer young when I began to till the soil in earnest, gardening has become a sometimes distressingly vapid philosophical activity for me. As I knelt beside the young spinach plants I remembered the odd question of a summer visitor; people say things here that they might be embarrassed to voice on the mainland.

"Do you pray a lot?" the visiting woman asked me, watching me weed. I have no memory of how I answered her at that moment but I was thinking to myself, beside the spinach, that we Island women do spend a lot of time on our knees. Perhaps "laborare" really is "orare," even though up in the bare little church nobody bends a knee to the Almighty, all glad to stand or sit for a change. Meandering ruminations brought to a halt by a sudden awareness that I was no longer alone. William's heavy footstep had made no sound on the grass, but, his shadow scarcely longer than mine, he was standing there behind me, silent, his craggy face suddenly gaunt.

"What's wrong?"

I straightened up, certain somehow that he brought bad

news, but not prepared for the truth. He couldn't find many words to tell it.

"It's Jenny... She was getting dinner, chopping up stuff for hodge-podge. Daniel went off to his building. He was only gone for ten minutes..." William was silent again, labouring to imagine those minutes.

"When he came back into the kitchen Jenny had cut her own throat, ear to ear, with the same damned sharp fish-knife she was using to cook with. Blood everywhere, and Jenny dead in the middle of it."

Daniel, distraught, had run across the road to Neighbour's place. She is everybody's neighbour, not just mine, and a large part of it is doing the dirty work, at any time of the day or night. Now she was up in Daniel's kitchen. They were waiting for the ferry, on a special run, to bring the undertaker. Jenny's bloodless body lay on the bed and Neighbour was on her knees scrubbing the reddened floor.

"It'll take her awhile, you can be sure of that." William half-shuddered despite the day's warmth. "Nothing you or the doc can do, anyhow. But I had to tell you."

He turned away and walked slowly back up the hill to wait alone in his house until Neighbour came home with her bucket and scrub brush. Does it really lighten the burden of pain to share it? We all tend to do it, anyhow, when it involves coming face to face with the one certainty we have in common, death.

* * *

Most of the funerals here are for old folk; they are buried in our cemetery even if they have died in the Old People's Home over the water. Should they be stricken when they are far away, Islanders who grew up on these few acres often ask that at least their ashes be buried here. The funeral director at Oldham merits our families' trust in his care and concern as he arranges things, and deals with the complications inherent in an "overseas" funeral — no hearse available, for instance. He knows who has a truck to lend, can find a couple of Oldham lads to go over for a day to dig the grave if the local boys are out fishing. With his round, open face and reassuring manner, he could have successfully managed many sorts of business, but he chose the one which will never lack customers, and he master-minds quite fitting ends to long lives. Since it is the custom here for the handsome coffin to be placed at the front of the church, family and friends can troop up the aisle in turn to say their farewells. In the porch as we left after old Josephine's funeral I heard one of her life-long friends say to another, with satisfaction, "You know, Josie hasn't looked so well for weeks." Her companion agreed, warmly. Perhaps they were both hoping they would look as good at the last.

Jenny's funeral was sadly different from most of them. Her death was shocking because it seemed unnecessary. Feeling low, she had crossed the water to see a doctor just a couple of days earlier, people said. He had given her some fancy new drug to raise her spirits, and then gone off on holiday without waiting to see how it suited her. Did it raise the knife to her quite young throat? That was the suspicion. After all, Daniel and Jenny were well set up in their good big house after years of excellent fishing, and the two good children, now grown up, were doing well on the mainland. Even though Jenny was never the chatty, cheery sort, *this* horror did not need to happen, everybody felt, just when she and Daniel could begin to take things a bit easier.

Years later, Daniel still talks of Jenny whenever someone will listen. He is restless now alone in his big house, lonely, and, crippled with arthritis, no longer able to fish. He keeps his garden and house ship-shape still, his kind children visit, but often he goes to the mainland for a few hours to take his mind off things. Once, recently, we came home on the same ferry, and when he noticed no old Jeep parked on the wharf, he called to me: "Want a ride up?" Gratefully I popped my parcels in his truck while he carted a huge sack of something over from the freight-box. Driving round the bay, bumping over the lunar craters caused partly by the water's relentless undermining of the sea-wall, I asked what on earth he had in the heavy sack on this October day.

"Why, food for the pheasants," said Daniel. "They come down around the house in the winter. I likes to watch 'em — pretty things."

He drove me, unnecessarily, off the road along the driveway right up to my back door, as he always does when he gives a lift, got out painfully to help with my parcels before going on to his empty house. God bless that gentle fisherman I thought as I lit the kitchen stove, and also the pheasants who please him.

Those birds delight me, too, when the Island lies under a deep carpet of snow. One January I watched the gaudy cock from up in our woods escorting his harem down the hill past the house. His five timid wives stepped daintily in single file ahead of him over the icy glitter, looking back now and then at their lord and master to make sure they were going the right way. I love them less when in late August the clever fellow brings the household down to the vegetable garden to devour the red and white currents and dig the early potatoes. They are very skilled at this work, denude the bushes and scratch the soil around the potato plants to expose the young tubers at which they peck away happily. Obviously, like me, they watch the calendar.

That particular harvester met his end and not through my intervention but because of yet another wild cat, prowling. We found his body near the potatoes, a few brilliant feathers scattered round it. Fortunately kind foreigners were visiting that day, with a young son. They organised a suitable burial up on the hill; it was necessary to dig a very long hole for the grave to accommodate the bird's tail.

As children, my younger brother and I buried fittingly numerous birds and small animals in our private cemetery in the wild part of the garden we grew up in; now I am happy to hand such obsequies over to younger generations.

Chapter 13

Updating a Wedding

*We could not have had a better dinner
had there been a Synod of Cooks.*
— Sam Johnson

What we thought at the time would be the grandest of all our Island gatherings (another came, unexpectedly, five summers later), the Golden Wedding, took place on a day which dawned as bright as that of the first ceremony, but the cloudless sky was about all they had in common. Instead of being contented peasants on a peaceful little island, we were in 1940 imprisoned, with millions of fearful people, in the south of a much larger one during what turned out to be the Battle of Britain. The Channel ports were barely twenty miles from the ancestral Hampshire village in which we were to be married, and we were hoping against hope that the knot could be tied before we all had to obey Churchill, grab pitchforks or something and fight on the beaches or in the narrow country lanes to beat back the expected German invasion. Hope grows like a weed in war-time, of necessity, and ours proved justified.

M.D. walked rapidly up the village High Street to the little church; until he was eighty he was incapable of moving slowly anywhere. Beside him trotted his Dandie Dinmont, his only Best Man, and on their heels a gaggle of local children entranced by the "Scotch Skirt" he wore for

Updating a Wedding

the occasion. The children and the dog waited docilely in the church porch while he took up his lonely post before the altar steps, fretting no doubt at the unnecessary delay; but the bride joined him only a few minutes later, properly escorted by her father. Papa had dug out his ancient slightly shiny dark suit, normally kept for funerals, and scarcely looked his tweedy plus-four country self; but he was probably glad to be handing me over to a good man — one fewer of the offspring to worry about.

Clothing being rationed, I was fortunate to have been able to salvage a short bolt of upholstery material from somewhere to make a dress for which no coupons were needed. Anything as frivolous and useless as a white satin gown was naturally out of the question, but there was in the village an old seamstress who cleverly, in three days and at a cost of one pound, outfitted me quite elegantly enough, if a little oddly. She worked from my measurements and a simple sketch I made of what the finished confection should look like — romantic little rounded train, lily-point sleeves, laced bodice — and sewed successfully. In every isolated village there are hidden geniuses, as there are on any small island.

As Papa and I proceeded decorously up the aisle I noticed that his suit smelt of moth balls and hoped that the scent of the garden flowers I had picked an hour earlier for my bridal bouquet would prove stronger; and I felt a little constrained and medieval in my upholstery, although actually I was simply striped vertically in a standard Regency green pattern used for chairs. In any case, that wedding dress was a splendid investment; with a few alterations, it lasted for twenty-five years. M.D.'s kilt met a sadder fate; as the war progressed and a couple of our children were born I cut it up to make warm clothing for them. There were six yards of good woollen cloth in it.

Travel being very difficult that summer there were few friends or relations in the pews; the younger ones were anyhow already dispersed in various corners of the globe. It was an Anglican church, though built solidly long before the Reformation, and of course still using the rich language of the old Book of Common Prayer. I was slightly taken aback by the fervour with which M.D. repeated the marriage vows after the stuffy old vicar, particularly the sentence: "With my body , I thee worship"; but the one endowing me with his worldly goods was simply funny. I knew he owned his kilt and his dog and nothing else since he was still a student and merely an aspiring M.D., just as he knew I had nothing. Papa, being an honourable late Victorian father, had informed him in a letter that I came with no dowry, nor even "expectations." We were to set out untrammelled by worldly goods of any sort.

Rapidly, cheaply and safely married we almost ran out of the church as the obliging organist thundered out, in a very rapid tempo, our chosen wedding march, "Santa Lucia." They said in the village that this old bachelor was the love-child of a village girl and a famous musician; he was certainly as good at helping Papa in the garden as he was on the organ. The local undertaker was waiting for us in the street; hearses being considered essential vehicles, I suppose, rated good gasoline rations. As we climbed in with the excited dog, but not the children, I could not help remembering Papa remarking wryly once that he preferred funerals to weddings — "at least one knows what's what at a funeral." I trusted that the combination of hearse, kilt and upholstery had made this ceremony bearable for him.

At the very small reception in my godmother's walled

cottage garden near the church, the refreshments, served under a canopy of roaring fighter planes, were meagre; although thanks to several village ladies who each donated an egg or an ounce of sugar or butter, we had a cake to cut. There was time for a small sip of champagne for each guest before the hearse squeezed down the lane again and whisked us several miles away to the nearest railroad station to catch the train for the first stage of our short honeymoon. We were going, with the dog and little else, to a remote island in the Hebrides, Iona, as far from the war as possible. It took us two days to get there, but the difficulties of the journey were forgotten as soon as we disembarked from the little boat on a blue and brilliant afternoon. We had reached an enchanted place, almost identical in its small size and variety of beaches and rocky cliffs to our present island on the other edge of the Atlantic; but its recorded human history stretched back to the sixth century and the arrival of St. Columba from Ireland.

I nearly died there, to the gentle sound of the rippling water — but not from bombs or invading Nazis. It was some unknown bug I had picked up in Europe in early 1939 which felled me. Time, not medicine, cured me; I did not leave my bones with those of the kings and monks and fishing folk, and M.D. did not have to write the difficult letter to my parents he feared would be necessary when my temperature reached 106°F. "Hyperpyrexia. Intractable. I am very sorry to have to tell you that Rachel only survived two weeks of marriage..."

* * *

Fifty years later, with many other narrow escapes long since half-forgotten, here we were, islanded again, but still together, remarkably intact, and ready to begin the last chapter of our lives with a suitable "bash" — or bang. No whimpering, anyhow.

By ten o'clock the crowd of guests had begun to assemble, probably not only to celebrate with us but also to forget their mainland lives for a few hours beyond the water. They packed the early ferry from Oldham but no one was in a hurry; the whole leisurely day lay ahead of them since she would not sail again until the evening. Sufficient this one day, perforce, for good or evil. People kept turning up all morning in their own small boats, and one graceful yacht caused a stir round the bay when she sailed in draped in flags and bunting. A few enterprising folk who had missed the ferry hitched rides on fish-boats returning home from Oldham.

Our canopy this time was not fighter squadrons but a spectacular striped marquee which the children (middle-aged now, of course) had rented and set up on the lawn where the band-stand now sits. In its shade was spread a lavish, unrationed meal put together by the daughter, daughters-in-law, their friends and Island women; the men had mixed buckets of Island wine, and numerous bottles of home-made champagne for the toasts waited under the trestle tables. Alerted about what was going on in the normal way, by notices posted earlier in the post-office and on the ferry, Islanders soon began to join the throng. Looking around at that odd crowd, sitting chatting on the grass, down on the beach with their children, enjoying the rose gardens or following the paths to the woods and headland, I knew it included people from all the many layers of our lives since we had exchanged the West Coast for the East thirty years previously; some who had worked with M.D. or me, strays who had crossed our paths, the occasional now very mature friend of our children, all now mingling with those we had found waiting for us on the Island when by chance we came exploring years before.

Last to arrive was a febrile little man with skimpy hair above a foxy face whom I had never seen before. He appeared suddenly on the lawn, moving rapidly amongst the knots of guests much occupied with talk, food, drink, towing behind him a strange and imposing woman. But if I at once concluded he was a gatecrasher with a boat, M.D. recognised him immediately, as well he should have; this was the fellow who had rescued him and saved the Lady Godiva from an early grave when she almost struck the rocks on the shore of a tiny island a few miles to the west of us a month previously.

Calmed and warmed after the near-calamity by a friendly drink with his saviour, M.D. was taken on a tour of inspection of the capacious new house sitting grandly in its own windswept domain. The entire island belonged to his emergency host, a Hungarian who had bought it so that he could peacefully indulge in the hobby to which he was passionately addicted — target shooting. He had set up a splendid range, and added to his chosen bliss by importing each summer a European companion who would both enjoy a sea-girt holiday and keep the house running for him. An island can be put to strange purposes if one is sole owner. In gratitude for interesting and helpful hospitality, M.D. before sailing off into the sunset had invited the man to our wedding party — and promptly forgotten all about him. Just another sailing adventure... I could not help but share M.D.'s desire to repay a boat-saving, perhaps even a life-saving, kindness, in however small a way. I know from long experience, some of it gained on other waters, why the houses on these shores have widow's walks. Women, by nature accustomed to waiting — for the birth of a child, the stew to simmer for hours, the buds to break, the harvest from the land — here must wait patiently also for a particular sail or boat silhouette on the horizon.

Night had hidden almost everything as I watched for the Lady Godiva that evening, knowing that, pretty creature that she was, she had no running lights — "Why should she?" M.D. would reason, "I won't be sailing at night. It would be a waste of money to fit her with them." I would silence my tongue, which wished to say, "But who knows where you'll be when night falls?"

It was falling then as I watched for the Lady Godiva. Phone calls came from around the bay as people noticed she was missing from her berth and the rosy light began to fade. Neighbour sent William down to watch with me. He had a sturdy boat he had built, with good lights on her, which he would take out on a search of the waters if necessary. But, "The Lady G. will be back before dark, you'll see," William asserted as he stood with me on the widow's walk "spying" the water, as he so often had before.

During these sunset sessions I was grateful for his company and the knowledge that his "life-boat" was standing by. However distractingly lovely the shimmering light over the water, my mind had the disturbing habit of going back over all the unlikely escapes from some near-fatal disaster at sea in one or other of the boats we had known. This resurrection of memories became even more painful, of course, on evenings when sudden squall clouds scudded across the sky or drifting June fog-banks rolled over the bay as William and I, in oil-skins, searched the west.

Updating a Wedding

M.D. was always an adventurous sailor, even as a child of ten navigating between the islands off the coast of B.C. Despite repeated near catastrophes, he remained a convinced optimist in this avocation as he did in every other area of his life. My own more realistic bent made me incapable of acting as his first mate — except on terra firma, where I was his first and last — and to his dismay I only sailed with him two or three times. Quite enough, I soon concluded, since "sailing willingness" had not been part of our war-time marriage contract and I would never get used to responding with instant obedience to shouted orders. However, feeling mildly guilty at my defection, I encouraged all five children to do their ship-board apprenticeship with their father; even the sensible mongrel dog they had for years learnt the necessary nautical terms, after she had been caught once or twice, in order to avoid being swept overboard by the boom as the boat came about. All the young became competent sailors, and for one of them at least his training saved not only his own life but also that of the eccentric polyglot captain and owner of a very old but well-built boat sailing from the Wash in S.E. England to France. The thrifty Canadian lad, at that time involved in his own educational tour of a good deal of the world, which came to include Africa and the Middle East as well as a year in India, hoped to save the cross-channel steamer fare by shipping out free, but skilled, on a private boat. However, the one he chose carried no radio, and when the worst hurricane in fifty years blew up the English Channel it was a surprise. At least two dozen grand yachts sank in those narrow waters before it blew itself out five days later, it was said afterwards. David, meanwhile, contrived to keep the old twenty-six-foot mahogany boat afloat in the towering house-high waves, fished his "captain" out of the wild billows when he was swept overboard, tried to comfort the man in his youthful way. The poor fellow had gone out of his mind with fear and was reduced to prayer. "Do you know the Pater Noster?" he shouted to David above the roaring wind and went down on his knees on the heaving deck, hoping to be prompted. David, cognisant of the prayer as well as the seas, brought boat and captain safely into harbour in the Channel Islands, whose astonished inhabitants looked after them for two days, warming and feeding them. The storm was finally dying as they sailed off, intact and refreshed, for Saint-Malo. A free crossing for the boy who was planning to work in France briefly; the peculiar "captain," in recognition of the fact that he owed his life to David, after they parted on French soil sent him a snap of the sturdy old boat, inscribed on the back with; "In thanks to David who saved my life."

William was right that evening, as usual. I had only mentally run through two or three near catastrophes and had not even reached the smashed mast one or the actual sinking when he pointed to a distant dot on the darkening water. "That's her all right." He smiled his slightly crooked smile and went off up the hill to Neighbour, his duty fulfilled. There was no breath of wind now — it usually dies with the sun — but the Lady Godiva limped home on her small motor in one piece. Another boat- or life-saving operation completed. David received a post-card as thanks; perhaps an invitation to a party was a step up in gratitude? There is anyhow, I gather, a different, more primitive, code at sea from that which operates on much of the land: every sailor assumes he is expected to rescue any other sailor in peril at whatever cost to himself; no thanks are necessary. The woman waits on her walk or "spying" through a sea-

Updating a Wedding

ward window and hopes that old code is working still on those restless waters as the light fails or the fog rolls in. "If it weren't for hope," as Neighbour says, "the heart would break."

Now, as M.D. and I stood together on the lawn surveying the festivities, he apprised me of the gate-crashers' identity and I made haste to approach the couple and welcome them. It was difficult to do this effectively because the woman was mute, having scarcely a word of the language spoken by the mainlanders in the crowd and being totally deaf to its more vivid Island version. It was plainly futile to try to introduce her to anyone; so the two of them merely ate and drank feverishly, after he had made his first circuit of the guests, looking, perhaps, for fellow target-shooters. When they had managed to smash four or five of the rented wine-glasses and were replete, they decided to leave.

"*Nem fontos*," I smiled pleasantly as I swept the broken glass off the deck, using the only two words I remembered from the distant months after our B.C. household unexpectedly doubled in size upon the arrival of six destitute refugees from the 1956 Hungarian Uprising. It was a useful phrase then: I hoped it was now, decades later. I think it means something like, "Aucune importance" or, "Don't worry yourself." In any case the strange couple sailed off as suddenly as they had arrived, the statuesque woman a proud figurehead on the deck, a fair breeze with them as they rounded the point.

As their boat disappeared, I noticed that we were being honoured with the presence of the Baptist minister. Dressed properly — this was the Sabbath, after all — in a dark suit and tie, he also didn't quite fit in with the rest of the guests. He took up his post close to the refreshment table, from time to time nibbling on one or other of the delicacies spread out there but of course not drinking. A long bony man with a nose to match, he watched the cheerful scene between bites of exotic chicken or "salade d'amour" with a puzzled and lugubrious air. I got the feeling that he had concluded that these were poor waters in which to fish for souls, which was after all his job in life. I knew he had given up on me a year before, when, coming down from an evening walk with his plump little wife on the paths M.D. had cut through our woods, he would find me weeding my vegetables on the cliff-top. Leaning on the wind-fence, he would admire my spinach or tomatoes, and his wife, not much taller than the fence, would smile in silent agreement. Then, before they went on their way back to the parsonage on the hill, a little above Neighbour's house across the road, he would say pointedly, "You do know what the times of service are, don't you?"

To make sure, he would reel them off. He always did his best to save my untormented soul, and no doubt many others. Toward the end of his tenure here, which was no longer than is usual, he was often on the mainland for days at a time. During these absences, when I suppose he was looking for a safe berth for his old age, Neighbour, not a constant church-goer but always a Samaritan, cared kindly for the large and tiresome parsonage dog. Church or no church, Neighbour's soul anyhow always struck me as saved; good works must count, the dog would agree.

Only the silent, smiling little wife accompanied the Minister on his hopeful mission that Sunday, and they left before the obligatory embarrassing toasts began. We were half-prepared for the inevitable by the astonishing arrival a couple of days previously of a fancy scroll signed by the

Updating a Wedding

Lieutenant-Governor of the Province congratulating us on having survived fifty years of marriage. Tax-payers' money is spent on odd things these days: who now could, or would want to, follow in our peculiar foot-steps?

A rambling little speech delivered by an elderly one-time colleague prompted M.D.'s succinct and lucid response detailing the major scientific and technological changes we had witnessed since 1940. Then we drank, after several others, a final toast to our one absent living son, thousands of miles away in the Northern Yukon, and the party proceeded in its own ragged and satisfactory way.

As I left the grateful shade of the marquee to go and talk to the old man who had been sitting alone in apparent contentment in a deck-chair on the cliff-top for a couple of hours, I passed two guests, who I knew had been enemies on the mainland once, engaged in an animated conversation. Both were smiling, the dauntingly tall and handsome Black as well as the mathematical Jewish genius: each had become a lawyer, now had something in common. In my mind's eye I could see the latter, aged about nine, sitting in the front row of one of my old classrooms long ago, relentlessly pestering me with unanswerable questions about such things as infinity. And it was not hard to recall some of our local problems when one or two Black Panthers from the U.S.A. visited these parts and borrowed my car. The sixties were a busy time for the Mounties; there were said to be subversives all over the place, and we merely gave them a little extra work as they felt obliged to tap our phone. Their attitude was understandable, since M.D.'s and my interests and extra-curricular activities were slightly suspect and our children were growing up and beginning to roam in foreign parts. One son, the hurricane survivor, was even receiving mail from *East* Germany, for heaven's sake; and no doubt they were well aware that he had also received a call from Interpol, from Cairo or somewhere. They were only gathering information, it turned out, not accusing the boy of some international crime. He was surprised to hear that the strange couple he had once hitched a ride with from Algiers to Egypt were wicked; he only knew that he had had a free ride, and that they would never have reached their destination if they had not taken him along with them. He knew how to keep an old jalopy running under dire, desert conditions, and they did not. And finally, our house seemed to harbour a drifting population of draft dodgers, deserters, and illegal immigrants. Plainly, we needed watching. I hope it all kept the phone-tappers happy; they were unlikely to learn of any treasonous plots, or indeed anything interesting at all. I spent considerable time in those days begging the younger inhabitants of the house to get off the phone so that I could deal with more serious matters, such as my work, over which they considered making assignations with a member of the opposite sex took precedence.

In fairness to the hard-working Mounties, I must add that, on the few occasions when an actual living R.C.M.P. officer turned up on our door-step looking for additional information, he was always mannerly, although I did heave a sigh of relief once when I was able, in all honesty, to respond [in the negative] to his question about whether a certain deserter was in the house. The lad was actually out sailing with M.D.: that evening the boat got stuck on a sandbar, so they didn't get back until the next day. Fortunately, that particular Mountie was not looking for the other illegal immigrant, a fellow from the Caribbean who was indeed in the house that afternoon. Time solves some prob-

Updating a Wedding

lems: one, the deserter, flew off to Sweden the following week, the other is now a respected professional out West.

Now, so long after the particular commotions of their, and our offsprings', youth, I caught a few words of the cheerful exchange between the two legal ex-enemies as I walked down to the cliff-top.

"You know," the one was saying to the other, "I still remember the talk you gave to the school about the Panthers, and I still think you were wrong." The breeze snatched his words away as I sat down on the grass beside the deck-chair, thinking to myself, "Perhaps it can even cure feuds on a day like this; there is surely no battle to be fought under this sun on such an island shore."

The Professor turned his eyes from the sea and tilted his straw hat back a bit on his massive head. He was mostly head, little neck, not much to the rest of him, although what there was was plumpish, since he was a skilled and fastidious bachelor cook. This was a man, they say, who was reading Shakespeare for pleasure around the age of seven and ready to graduate from Harvard or some such place around the age of sixteen.

In another life, on the mainland, I sometimes listened to him debate or lecture and was always entertained. His thoughts emerged in a deliberate string of enormously long and intricate sentences, each one a fugue of interjectory phrases and elaborating clauses piled up in a crescendo of exact meaning. One shifted uncomfortably on the hard auditorium bench, wondering whether this time he really was lost in the maze of thought and there could be no end to the sentence. But calmly, invariably, he struck the resolving chord, and comprehension dawned. The last time I had seen him was by chance, on a shopping trip on the mainland. We were both pushing our grocery carts as we greeted each other, and I remembered that, now retired, he had recently undergone triple by-pass heart surgery.

"Remarkably successful," he said, and went on to detail, at some length, the extraordinary experience it had been.

In parting, I glibly called to him, "Look thy last on all things lovely, every moment…" He turned, and for once uttered a short, simple sentence.

"Who wrote that?"

The author's name was one of the few things I knew which the Professor didn't, and it was probably due, like any such others, to my having grown up on other continents. It was Walter de la Mare, who died, I think I can attest, at eighty-three in 1956. I heard that he was a wonderful travelling companion on the top of a London double-decker bus or indeed anywhere else, and I can believe it. A multifarious mind, a man who always looked his last, on moon or roses, or, in prose, into the mysterious recesses of the human mind in *The Return* or *Memoirs of a Midget*; and who was fascinated all his long life by islands.

On that curious afternoon, having ceased "looking his last" on the whispering wavelets, as he began his critique of M.D.'s response to the toast, the old Professor inevitably brought with him a whiff of academe to float with the salty air around us.

"Of course he was right about the invention of antibiotics, reserved initially to curb the spread of venereal diseases amongst the military, as we later learnt, and about certain other astonishing developments which have changed the face of the globe since 1940. But he was wrong about…and he omitted any mention of…"

Of course he was and did. M.D. saw the world through

the eyes of a dedicated scientist with a microscope on the laboratory bench in front of him, and probably an interesting cadaver waiting in the morgue downstairs. Immediate, urgent work; although forensic autopsies could occasionally lead him beyond the hospital confines to wider horizons. A drowned woman was washed up once on a shore on the other side of the province. Did someone push her in? How had the corpse reached that particular part of the coast? What ocean currents operated there? Determining its provenance required a few happy days of field-work for the pathologist, studying the currents and tides in the area. The Mounties, of course, were allies in those simple days before our children grew up when M.D. was still very much "*persona grata*" with them, very useful in their work.

    The Professor in the deck-chair, no "pure" scientist but a sociologist and educator with his own horizons, naturally had a different perspective on the last fifty years. Neither man's, of course, agreed with mine, though both educated me. When the war pounced on Europe I was barely twenty and it exonerated me from having seriously to pursue some academic discipline or other; I was free to dabble here and there for the rest of my life, quite undisciplined.

    I left the Professor in the company of the two youngish people who had joined me on the grass beside his chair, ex-students of his. He was stringing together another of his lengthy verbal necklaces as I slipped up to the house to check on the plumbing, something a hostess has to keep an eye on in these parts when an unlikely crowd descends. Our well is the best on the Island, only twelve foot deep but fed by three springs. Less fortunate folk used to line up with buckets in summers of drought to draw from it, Neighbour says. Bread humans can wait for, but not water. Nowadays, with fancy plumbing in the house, the springs are quite fully occupied. They never let us down — always a bath available when we come in grubby from land or sea, always crystal clear water from the tap in the kitchen. But when crowds descend from the mainland one must consider the blessed well's deep and simple pulse.

When I "spied" with the binoculars the number of mainlanders the ferry had brought that Sabbath morning as they disembarked, I quickly penned a small notice to tack to the bathroom door. "Please flush only when essential. Perhaps men could use the woods or the beach round the point?" I knew, of course, that Island guests would have thought ahead.

In the old days, Neighbour says, the outhouses were the women's preserve. No doubt they were satisfactory places to retreat to for conversation and privacy to complain about the men's outrageous behaviour. No armchairs; although I did once see a comfortably padded three-holer by a house on the loop-road some years ago. The one we inherited was a modest and bare two-holer, which disintegrated soon after we led the water into the house: people with less faithful wells wisely kept theirs in good repair against times of drought.

There was a short and cheerful queue outside the bathroom, all women, and a young father was reading the notice on the door to his two small sons; puzzled but obedient, they followed him out into the sun and up to the woods. I was relieved to find that the three little springs were still doing their duty: M.D. would admire my prescience as a hostess, surely. Following the males out through the west door, I looked around but could see no sign of him; probably he had gone off with some of the company up to the headland. The Professor was still dispensing wisdom from

Updating a Wedding

his deck-chair to his ex-students, little knots of people meandered around chatting on the lawn, and from down on the beach occasional joyful shouts floated up: children were finding treasures.

Kindly relieved by age from unnecessary activity — one never lacks the necessary here — I placed a lone chair in the small shadow of the widow's walk, and gratefully noticed that the indefatigable young continued to dispense food and drink to guests under the striped marquee, and that William had taken up his station with them. I trusted he was helping himself as well as them. Luella, I saw as I relaxed in the shade, was engaged in conversation with a mainland friend of mine, a pleasant woman who has become an expert in one of the newer "disciplines," gerontology, although she is far from old herself. Neighbour was down in the sunken garden with some mainland woman, talking roses no doubt, not old age.

Luella looked somewhat puzzled as she politely tried to answer the interested foreigner's questions, but she also looked very elegant in her party clothing, a flowered dress and a wide straw hat on her white hair. (All the Islanders had turned up dressed in their best: it was a wedding of sorts, after all, wasn't it? The mainlanders, of course, were celebrating by wearing their oldest jeans and T-shirts.) Fragments of the difficult conversation between the baffled old Luella and the middle-aged expert reached me. It takes more than an afternoon to discover how Island women manage to survive so long, I was thinking; and none of them fit into any neat modern sociological pigeon-hole.

My mind wandered back to a charming old Lebanese merchant who came to my rescue years ago in the city. I was searching for an apparently unobtainable replacement part for Jacob's ancient woodstove; this little store was my last hope. Elbows on the wooden counter of his small but flourishing business, his lined old Middle-Eastern face cheerful with memories of earlier days, the little man told me what was required then for a foreigner — anybody at all from over the water — to be accepted on the Island. He had arrived on this continent before the last war, a destitute immigrant. To survive, he became an old-fashioned peddlar, selling his small stock of wares in rural districts of the province. Beginning to prosper because he gave good value for hard-earned money and sold useful stuff, he began to wonder whether perhaps he could expand his market beyond the mainland to the handful of inhabited off-shore islands, and soon contrived a marine lift to ours.

"You had to wait until they knew you could be trusted," he told me. But within six months: "It was chowder or hodgepodge for lunch in some woman's kitchen whenever I got off the boat... Sometimes my wife came with me. She liked the Island, too." He smiled, remembering her and their joint excursions. Too soon — I could have listened to the old boy's reminiscences all afternoon — he went off to find the precious stove-part hidden in a box somewhere. "Five dollars," he said, plunking the peculiar bit of metal down on the counter. Worth far more to this customer: a lame stove is a sad thing in a kitchen.

His sons have inherited the odd eclectic business. As I drive by the little store-front in an unfashionable neighbourhood these days, on my way somewhere or other, I notice gratefully that they still sell brightly coloured pictures of Lebanese saints as well as stove parts, and hope that the local Lebanese community continues to patronise them. Their father was not the only double-foreigner — one of

Updating a Wedding

those who have travelled other thousands of miles from other continents before they cross our seven-mile-wide moat. They often fit in better here, being used to watching and listening in order to survive, than do the North Americans who imagine the Island is merely a backward addendum to the mainland. The latters' simple modern lexicon seems to have taught them that a "community" is a group of like-minded people, easy to get along with. We know that for Islanders it signifies everybody marooned with you on a dot in the implacable ocean.

Sitting peacefully in the shadow of the widow's walk, I watched the blonde teen-aged granddaughter in her blue party dress industriously running from group to group of the visitors, gathering their signatures in the guest-book, and congratulated myself on at least having dealt with the essentials for the day — water for the bathroom, and the weather. When I had woken at 2 a.m. that morning untidy ribbons of cloud were streaming across the face of the almost full moon; appalled at the vision of the expected army of invaders compressed for shelter from summer storms within the small house, I put up the necessary prayers. They were answered by dawn, sky and reflecting sea an unsullied blue. Fire in the woods being of no concern today, after last week's heavy rains, just this small patch of peaceful earth remained. The people temporarily wandering on it would provide sufficient quiet entertainment for this old woman and might find enough for themselves.

The voices of the children floated up from the shore, a few Islanders had joined Neighbour and were still mingling with a group of mainland gardeners down in the rose garden; the Island ladies have always taken a proprietary interest in my bushes. And not far from my chair but out in the sun sat the widowed mother of several children our own younger ones had grown up with in another, mainland, life.

"The horrors are here waiting for you," I would shout up the stairs to ours when two or three of her kids appeared on our city doorstep; no doubt Frances did the equivalent when ours turned up round the corner on hers. One of our boys, at the age of seven — hence of wisdom, perhaps he had heard — lectured her several times on proper methods of disciplining the young: he believed hers suffered unduly and would resent her no-nonsense Scottish approach to education. Frances, smiling, thanked the boy for his advice, and continued along her own path. Time has proved the seven-year-old expert wrong; her children still love her unconditionally, it seems. Three of them were sprawled on the grass beside her now, watching with amusement as the elderly toast-proposer approached their mother; he had been doggedly following her around all day. Emboldened by wine and sun he was plainly set on taking one more shot at charming her into accepting a date with him. One could understand his perseverance; the poor fellow was facing a lonely old age, his wife having left him a few years previously; and this woman was something to write a poem about. She was a visual tonic to anyone meeting her thirty-five years ago when we were neighbours, not a detail wrong on that well-boned, open face. Now she was even more strikingly agreeable to look at, hair white but abundant, eyes the same far-seeing blue, merely smile-wrinkles round them to betray the age of that clear complexion. It was a tranquil face which glowed with her own brand of Scottish good-sense and Italian earthiness; she had lived in both countries as well as this one, and learnt from each. And widowhood had not diminished her.

Her pursuer brought up another chair and placed it

hopefully beside Frances. Her children graciously went off to chat with long-lost friends, leaving their mother to parry his earnest appeals with her smiles. Was he picturing, as he talked and sipped more wine (she had wisely refused another glass) what it might be like to sit across the breakfast table from that lovely face each morning? She told me later that she never did go out with him, but had greatly enjoyed the sun and sea of that day anyhow.

The sun was sinking noticeably lower when I caught sight of M.D., followed by a gaggle of guests, ambling down the hill path. He was moving, courteously, with unaccustomed slowness because his companions kept insisting on stopping to pick berries or gather wild-flowers. Looking at my watch I decided it was time to ring the old school-bell to summon any stragglers in woods or meadow or round the shore; its cheerful clang carries far beyond a shout. No more than the tide, the ferry waits for no man or woman, and I had no intention of imposing further on the well with perhaps twenty overnight houseguests. It was entitled to twelve hours of rest.

Obediently — amazing the power of an unexpected bell — the morning crowd gradually re-assembled on the lawn before setting off in dribs and drabs along the dusty bay road to the wharf; a few of the more aged bravely accepted a taxi drive from M.D., an attentive host as ever, in the spluttering Jeep.

Every guest seemed to have caught the ferry as she sailed away fully laden and on schedule, under a still blue sky on barely ruffled water, thank God. They hung over the railings on the upper deck to wave good-bye to this small island. It was not Crusoe's, the Swiss Family's, or any more exotic one; but maybe it had granted them a small respite in their complicated mainstream lives.

A couple of hours later our young and their allies had completed the demolition of the striped marquee; it had been a unique landmark while it lasted, no such contraption having ever been seen by fishing boats round these shores before. As the western sky hinted that it was about to flame in glory, our helpers also sailed off, in two little vessels, bearing with them, as a meagre reward for their labour, left-over victuals and a little wine. The last member of the party to leave was the youngest, the three-month-old granddaughter. She was still smiling in her sleep as she went aboard in her mother's arms. I was too, in an attenuated way, as I waved good-bye. No old woman smiles as the infant does, untrammelled by experience. I used to think as a young woman that the essence of comfort and joy visible on the face of a small dreaming child was what enabled mothers to survive the miseries of rearing children. Only get over the current hurdle, hunger, a sudden fever, acute frustration, and the child will smile that unadulterated smile again.

Apart from the patent disappointments of the Minister and the widow's suitor, the guests seemed to have left contented. Perhaps even the bibulous target-shooter and his lady had? It appeared to have been a rather fortunate wedding day. Moreover, I didn't even have to get upholstered for this one; a half-price cotton dress and three-dollar hat from the nearest bargain-basement to replace my normal work clothes sufficed. (They have never been worn since: they hang at the back of a cupboard as historical artifacts now — less adaptable than the first sturdy wedding garment.)

The sun completed its day's journey, the little breeze gave up until tomorrow; we Islanders were left in moonlit silence.

Chapter 14

Zucchinis and Forestry

*One tree falling makes more noise than
a forest growing.*
— Chinese saying

"You know," said Della, sitting down, weary, on the cabin bench opposite me after a bit of shopping in Oldham, "you know, whenever I sees you I thinks, 'Zucchinis!'"

Zucchini Rachel — one could earn a less attractive title. Looking across at that kindly, brave face, its wrinkles deepened by her smile, I told her I thought "Cucumbers!" whenever we met. I had not forgotten how years ago she ran out from her garden in the South Cove waving her arms frantically to stop the old Jeep as it rattled by. We came to a halt quickly — the brakes were efficient in those days — but were somewhat worried. Another catastrophe? The last time we had taken that bit of road we were flagged down by the son of an old fisherman; the fellow and his grown boys had been about to launch their boat for another trip out when he was felled by a heart attack. He was lying on the stony beach, his head cushioned by the orange life jacket the sons had slipped under it. There was nothing M.D. could do. The sudden widow, called from their cottage, stood at her husband's feet, her apron thrown up over her face, keening, a silhouette against the cloudless sky, the rippled water.

When Della caught us, though, it was good news. She had grown a huge crop of cucumbers that year owing to the wonderful summer and didn't know what to do with them all. Couldn't we use some? Of course we could, loaded up the back seat of the Jeep, and went home to make our first Island pickles, having gathered a hint or two from Neighbour on how to set about it. Reluctant cook as I am it was not beyond me.

Della remains cheerful despite being herself a widow and having watched her daughter die young, leaving small grandchildren whom their grandmother had to help raise. Fortunately she has fine sons near Oldham who come over the water to help her in any emergency. They have even taken time to come to my rescue once or twice, with the greatest of courtesy. Good boys, as Della says, even if they are now in their forties. We chatted a bit that day on the ferry, then she smiled again and finished, as courteous as her sons: "And now I'll hold my tongue. You'll be wanting to get to that book on your knees. But don't go ruining your eyes now. All that reading you do…you'll be wearing them out."

As a small child I rashly ignored exhortations not to strain my eyes by reading in bed. That sort of behaviour, it was said, drove Milton blind; but even after I had been told to memorise the sonnet on his blindness, I fear I persisted in this dangerous, now lifelong, habit. Some risky behaviour is perhaps essential to an interesting life; unwittingly, at seven years of age, I think I chose sensibly. Nevertheless, I greatly appreciate Della's neighbourly concern. Once we approach seventy we all watch the bits of us which may be wearing out, and I do now consider carefully what I will read and stash away in my attic, refuse to waste small time

Zucchinis and Forestry

on ephemeral pages.

The zucchinis, which I began to grow once my vegetable garden was in full swing and there was an odd corner to pop a few foreign seeds in, proved to be a fool-proof crop whatever the weather. Della noticed their different-looking leaves one day when she was over to the cliff-top, and I did some propaganda for its ease of cultivation, usefulness in a dozen dishes, including jams and bread. The following summer several of the women bravely began to grow this innovative plant; it knew how to produce and how to behave, and I heard no complaints. But when, with some enthusiasm, I introduced Jerusalem artichokes topped by their sunny flowers, the response was cool, even though this was something the sensible native peoples had enjoyed for hundreds of years before the Europeans turned up in these parts. The unique taste was not popular, and, if one rashly planted a few tubers, they tended to take over the entire garden. I have long since segregated mine now in their own limited precinct; but of course I have more land, Jacob's land, to play with than most of the women with their smaller patches.

By and large, naturally, I am the one who has benefitted most from communal sharing. I had more to learn, the women more to teach, and sometimes the men; they all have an ancestral knowledge of our small land. An ignorant newcomer, I have appropriated much necessary information from our neighbours, used some of it immediately, tucked the odd bit away for future reference, things such as the tid-bit Martin gave me one day. We all know that good fences make good neighbours, but I was not aware that good fences depend on the posts being cut two days before the dark of the moon. That's what his grandfather had told him, Martin said, when asking if he could cut a few trees on our land one February. A bit more wisdom for my cluttered mental attic, to be filed alongside the Touareg proverb, *"Rapprochez vos coeurs, éloignez vos tentes,"* and Neighbour's encouraging saying, "When the tree is big enough to bend, you know it will survive." (My classification system is marvellously haphazard and would horrify M.D., had he access to it, his own files being thoroughly scientific.)

Those words of Neighbour I brought out when I was first seized by a minor attack of tree-planting frenzy. I was hoping to replace some of the fine hardwoods which the original settlers here had felled to build their homes and warm them. A little later, of course, when those pioneers took to the water, some of that wood sailed out to sea in the hulls of their boats. This tiny island in due course became famous for the designing-genius and craftsmanship of our men. "How did you come to build boats?" one of our best-known boat-builders was asked once. He thought back through the long years behind him and answered wryly: "Well, when you live on an island you might want to get off it sometimes, you know..." Necessity, invention. Not all inventions are as benign and beautiful as those created under primitive conditions in our boat-shops.

By the time we had found our home here, there was scarcely a hardwood left; one magnificent copper beech on the east hill, the odd clump of graceful silver birch inland. The cheeky little "mink" spruce had taken over almost everywhere and were invading many of the old pastures.

When the young trees ordered from the Forestry Department duly arrived on the ferry and I opened the box, it was plain that there would be a long wait before they were tall enough to bend with the wind and thus survive. They were minute, barely nine inches high; but the bill was very

Zucchinis and Forestry

small too so I was not about to complain. Instead, I bent my own back for several days digging out suitable niches in the rocky sod up our hill, round the meadow and the Dell, for the infant trees. My frenzy assuaged, I pressed a few leftovers in the box on William. The sun had retreated behind a bank of low cloud when I decided to retreat myself with tired muscles to the house and knocked on Neighbour's door. William graciously accepted the orphans and carefully planted them on his land the following day, even though it was a rainy one.

Now, years later, there are many ten- and twelve-foot-tall survivors, oaks and maples, all over the place. They have learnt to bend with the weather, as we all must. But I cheated a bit when I splurged and bought a few other trees already four-foot high, reared gently in some mainland nursery: a couple of Welsh "fairy-trees," Mountain Ash, rich with berries the birds love in the fall, crab-apples, a clump of silver birches, a black locust. And I was a little envious when Neighbour rescued and successfully transplanted a six-foot-high Laburnum from Oldham. It had grown beside the tiny cottage there of a cousin of hers, whose death had caused the sale of the little old place. Now it flourishes in her backyard, near the well, and begins to approach the size and beauty of one I knew as a child in England. Here I think it is fittingly called "Golden Rain"; and delicate as it looks, it is plainly tough enough to stand up to our winds from the sea. Names are apt to change as plants and people wander over the globe; dandelions, which are said to have travelled far and wide in the dust on the boots of British Empire builders, probably have a dozen besides "pissenlits," and zucchinis I know for sure are also "courgettes."

"Do no harm," I said to myself as I planted my trees,

remembering the Hippocratic Oath which M.D. and his fellow graduates took without a second thought not so long ago. A simple command, it seemed then; but for a physician today, mired in the modern quagmire of medical ethics, impossibly complex. And as for my humble forestry project, of course I harmed the young spruce in the interest of the hardwoods. I ruthlessly pull them up always; if I let them have their way they would march down the land with their numerous progeny right up to our doorstep, and peer in at every south-facing window.

Things were clearer for a couple of serious tree-planters of whom I knew. One was a man who spent the latter part of his life trudging alone over vast areas of southern France re-planting the great forests which had been destroyed by monstrous fires one summer. He must have died happy, knowing he had done something not only incontrovertibly harmless but actually helpful for the endless stretches of mountainous land — and their human and animal inhabitants. The other one who came to mind was the very young man who set about repairing some of the damage done centuries before he was born, not by fire but by man, to the lower slopes of the Atlas Mountains rising behind Sétif, a small settlement in Algeria. Roman invaders had planted their familiar olives there, but the land was too acid for them and they did not long survive the Empire; the flanks of those mountains had remained bare and brown for many centuries. (One of the servants of that empire dropped a small coin from his pay not far away; it lay there in the sand until by chance young David picked it up. The head of the Emperor Constantine was still clearly visible on it.) The lad had already spent a few months in the village before the idea of re-forestation hit him, and by then he had been accepted into the community on account of various other provenly useful things he had done. These included providing a demonstration of how to build a small, safe, cooking stove from clay. For hundreds of years the women had cooked on tiny open fires, into which the infants slung on their backs had a habit of tumbling now and again as their mothers bent to stir a pot. When the head man of the place asked David to build a stove for him, everybody else wanted one, and all was plain sailing for further undertakings. In due course, sixty-three thousand young Aleppo pines arrived from France, and the whole population turned out for a carefully organised group planting-party. It lasted for a month, but the arduous work was completed just before the necessary rains came. Probably a few babies were spared serious burns by that foreigner's brief presence in the village; certainly the mountain flanks, and hence the water-table, benefitted. Those thousands of young trees swayed as necessary and survived; when David passed through some years later, in 1968, on his way to Tanzania for a summer's work, the slopes were green as far as the eye could see. What is life like now in re-forested Sétif after further years, not of destructive Romans but of Algerians fighting Algerians? "All's to do again," often if not always, as any housewife or gardener knows; but not all the pundits.

Destruction for the land may come naturally, through the cycles of disease, hurricanes, lightning-fires; or of course we humans may be the immediate cause of disaster. There was an August evening when we ourselves came close to destroying not only my modest forestry project up the hill, round the meadow and the Dell, but the rest of the Island too. The magnificent red fire-engine which crossed the water with much fanfare and lived in the basement of the Centre for several years had gone back whence it came; now we no longer had enough volunteers to man the thing.

The night of our fiery near-catastrophe we had gone to bed with the sun. It was one a.m. when the phone rang; sleepy after a hard day's work, I was put out at being woken so unkindly. Who on earth could be calling at such an ungodly hour? Our Yukoner? Or was it an Islander needing M.D.'s kind advice about whether they should call the ferry for a mercy run to get some old person, suddenly taken ill, to the hospital quickly? If necessary he would accompany the patient on the stretcher to the "main." (He had donated one to the Island years ago, and it was still stored in the basement of the Centre.)

"Don't like to bother you," said Dorothy's voice from across the bay, "but I couldn't sleep tonight… I was sitting looking at the water. Did you know that fire you had on the beach today had taken off again?" We had been cleaning up and burning brush all afternoon down on our westward beach where Jacob used to make his bonfires.

"Good God!" I was wide awake now. Through the window I could see that the fire had already leapt up over the high cliff-top and was running through the dry grass on its way to the headland woods; the flames from the rock fireplace flared twelve feet high.

"Thought I'd send Victor across to help…" Dorothy ended; but she no doubt continued to "spy."

Her lad, loping over, was here in a wink, the men in our household (we had a son visiting) pulled on pants and rushed out in horror, the daughter-in-law and I, in our nighties but with buckets, joined them; I blessed the well which allowed us to keep them filled. It was a warm night, perfectly suited to scantily clad fire-fighters, but it had also been very calm, no spray that evening on the wide flat rocks at high tide to ensure that we had completely killed the bonfire earlier. Through all our frantic activity the little granddaughter slept at peace up in the moon-lit attic; at four it is only one's own discomfort or nightmares which wake one, but her father stayed up until dawn, patrolling the cliff-top every half-hour lest some treacherous spark should spring into life again — a slight shift in the breeze could mean the end of our house, Neighbour's, and many others, as well as the woods. Victor had considered that all was safe by 3 a.m. and loped off home, rightly confident that there was no more need to fuss. Back in my bed, after all that healthful exercise with the buckets, I fell asleep thinking that insomnia has its uses. Dorothy's, anyhow, was a blessing to us across the bay that night; and so was her lad.

Chapter 15

The Laws of Which Land

Does no one read the Highway Code?
Most people drive without a care
right in the middle of the road —
though they can see I'm driving there.
           — Piet Hein

Not long after we came here Ethel told me that Jacob's land, now ours, could be planted a week or more earlier than her and Pete's patch; theirs lies somewhat higher and further from the water on the loop road, the route I take when returning from the store in order to glimpse her riot of flowers. Since our home is quite close to the Island post-office, friends who have walked over to pick up their mail sometimes cross the road and seek me out on the land; our gardens are a bond between us. One sun-filled July day Ethel came to check on my progress and found me on the cliff-top amongst the thriving vegetables. "I see you've wed it," she said, approvingly. "It looks as though those weeds don't stand a chance with you around." Words here still often derive their form from the first language of the old settlers, but Ethel was right in both meanings of that one: I had indeed just finished weeding the garden, and I was indeed married to it, after an educational period of engagement. But she was wrong to assume that it always looked so tidy. The local knowledge has saved me scarce time and wasted work — the right moment to plant, which seeds have stood the test of time, hints on Island weather, and possible disasters to watch for.

Each spring, in these parts a mere gasp of two or three weeks between winter and summer, we women grow restive with the desire to get the growing started, but one must obey the Natural Law of the land, however small its compass. Whenever I was tempted to ignore what my neighbours taught me, a vision of the vast collective farms of Eastern Europe assailed me. We saw some of them in the early 1980s, stretching efficiently to the horizon on either side of the road as we drove from Budapest to the Turkish border. Once, they say, certain brilliant Moscow bureaucrats figured out a way to increase the year's yield of potatoes in one of the Baltic States by offering rewards to those farms which planted earliest, a rational incentive in the view of the distant experts in their offices. The result, of course, when some poor dolts took the bait, was a disaster which greatly astonished the powers that were. There was no "positive reinforcement" after a pathetic crop. Nature, in all her particularities, will not be hurried by government fiat; and she will inevitably take her revenge in due course on the huge western agribusiness corporations trying to fool the soil in pursuit of efficiency and gold. Even were the experts to find a way to bio-engineer a New Man, it is hard, if one has lived through most of this century, to believe they can contrive a New Earth. It is complicated stuff, I think as I dig the loam and watch what springs from it. We cannot change its laws on a whim, however expert we may think we are; those who live and work on it are the most likely to understand and respect its ways. And it cannot be genetically engineered overnight, or even in nine months.

A Treasured Island

The other law of the land, which operates beyond the water, was designed to deal not with the eternal behaviour of plants, soil and sea but with the strange behaviour of human beings, and currently the familiar framework within which it tries to function seems to shift and wobble every few months. For perhaps a hundred and fifty years the Island managed to deal not only with the land and the water but also with the vagaries of the human settlers without looking to the mainland for help. In any small and isolated community people had a chance not only to know each other but to find ways, however imperfect, to put up with each other. According to old Sam Johnson, civilisation consists in civility; he found no need to put the former word in his dictionary. Here there was just enough of the latter around to keep our minuscule civilisation running smoothly, most of the time. Clandestine transgressions, such as stealing or vandalism, would be difficult to achieve, anyhow, on our few acres.

The house we moved into in 1971 had stood empty but fully furnished for four years but nobody had broken into it nor taken anything from the outbuildings, not even the tempting nearly full bottle of rum very visible on a window-sill. Perhaps the Law of the Eye discouraged would-be miscreants; there would always be someone idly "spying" round the bay or from up the hill. And perhaps that law was buttressed by the Law of the Ear, especially after the new-fangled telephone reached our shores. For years we shared party-lines with three or four other people, who could eavesdrop on our chatting if they were so inclined. Probably it was during those early phone days that some local poet pronounced the words:

The Laws of Which Land

God knows all,
Fred's all nose.

No doubt Fred had time to listen to the humming phones as well as to "spy," whoever he was or wasn't. Of course there was the odd moment when the indigenous safeguards failed. They say that one moonless night a century ago old Ned wheeled his barrow down the steep hill from his cottage and tipped it into the bay. In the morning his wife's body was found floating there, her hair spread out like wispy white seaweed on the water. Some wondered whether she was alive or dead when Ned disposed of her, but he, like her, was well past eighty; at that age he was not likely to get a new wife and repeat the operation, whatever it was, was he? A reasonable supposition. Nobody sailed over to the mainland to fetch that Law, and Amy was decently buried anyhow.

The land-feuds and the inheritance ones had a tendency to simmer on quietly down the generations but they seldom erupted. When I make my little detour to glimpse Ethel's flower-garden I first must pass an interesting old house on the other side of the road until lately shared by two elderly brothers. One of them kept his half of the fine square old building spruced up regularly with new white paint; the other fellow didn't bother himself with upkeep, so the place developed a pie-bald look. It was said that the two men never spoke to each other, which caused sorrow to friends of ours. They had noticed an attractive little old cottage in the other cove standing empty and wanted to buy it. These youngsters, who were almost another son and daughter to us since we had known them for ages, had always been the best sort of guests whenever they visited with their children, working ones, helpful on the land. Now they wanted to become Islanders themselves; the father was a teacher, could take over our little school, he hoped. When they enquired about buying the deserted cottage, however, their dream fell apart. The pretty cottage with its own view of the water was another piece of the silent brothers' joint inheritance, and since they were unable to communicate with each other there could be no agreement for its sale. Within a few years, therefore, it simply "rottened down" into the earth. (Neighbour and I are well aware these days that we, and our men, are also "rottening down" even though we are much younger than that well-built little dwelling was; bones are not as strong and long-lived as good timbers are, but both require a modicum of care to carry on. That cottage was granted none).

We have now all graduated to private phones, but of course simultaneously our privacy, even if it was less absolute than that of those two silent brothers, has been invaded lately in far less human ways than in the past, and much more effectively. The many agencies of government and business, thanks to modern technology, have got each one of us citizens "taped" right down to the number of pills our mainland doctor may have told us to take each day as well as to how our credit rating stands and what sorts of things we are likely to buy, how we might vote. Progress and prosperity bring their own problems. "Give a beggar a horse," says an ancient Shropshire proverb, "and he will ride to the devil": give any of us everything we can be induced to want in the way of horse-power and modern gadgetry and we may all do likewise, whether or not we recognise that we too are beggars.

* * *

The Laws of Which Land

Winds from the mainland have been freshening for sometime; it was probably the one which brought us the influence of T.V. which in the end led to the grand meeting up in the Centre. This gathering was organised by a group of the older folk who had become so upset that they called the Mounties at Oldham complaining about the noise and the danger the reckless young people were creating with all their vehicles, brought over as near wrecks from the "main" and cleverly repaired by the new owners. Couldn't the Law do something about this growing problem? The old people themselves felt powerless: this generation didn't give a damn for their elders any more.

The Recreation Centre, a symbol in itself of changing times, was built a few years after we came here, across from the school, and is equally utilitarian architecturally. Until it went up with the help of our local carpenters (every man here is a skilled carpenter, and some of the women), wedding parties and such celebrations were held in an ancient barn high up on the east hill with a fine view over the bay, and the young people found their week-end fun at Gus's little place. He opened his two-room home to them on Saturday evenings, and for an entrance fee of twenty-five cents per customer they could listen to old records on his wind-up phonograph, even dance a bit. Gus's law forbade liquor but everybody seemed to have a good time, including, no doubt, the host. He is the Island's efficient electrician and plumber, although he did not bother to squeeze a bathroom into his own tiny home, nor even put in a telephone; and he is also general gadget repairman, supplier of modern appliances, the entrepreneur who markets on the mainland the summer savoury the women grow. (Summer slavery they call it; it is tedious work tending and preparing the stuff).

A Treasured Island

He runs the fish and chips stand on the road to the wharf during the summer months, hiring one or two sensible youngsters to help him; and they say that in his youth he even taught school for a year on a neighbouring island. A man of many parts, about the only thing he never got involved in was fishing; he has always gone his own way, kept his thoughts to himself under his wild curly aureole of now greying hair, and never gossiped. He is as necessary to the Island in his own way as Neighbour is, even though they have little in common except deep concern about the way the new world is going, and a strand of wisdom which allows them to stand back from local disputes such as land-feuds. It does no good to take sides when everybody is partly wrong, which is usually the case.

The Centre is now where wedding festivities take place, school concerts, gatherings after a funeral, interesting sales of various sorts which even lure mainlanders over for a day to buy the quilts and mats and so on which the women have worked over the winter months, and "showers" for a bride-to-be or a mother-to-be, with plenty of amusing games for the guests — all women, of course — to play, as well as gifts for the honouree, and, inevitably, food. The women's committee puts on a fine feast for any occasion; long tables are spread with a wide variety of favourite home-grown Island dishes, you help yourself to all you can manage and find congenial companions at one of the score of smaller tables round the walls with whom to eat it. The Centre is also the scene of regular card and bingo parties, it is where we duly vote at election time, and, of course, it is where the young now congregate on weekends to dance to the music of the noisy rock groups who cross the water to play for them. Gus is not there to keep the Law in his silent way, and

The Laws of Which Land

I imagine it costs more than twenty-five cents for the evening's entertainment.

In due course the mainland Law, in the shape of four smartly uniformed officers, puttered over to the Island in their small boats to do their best to solve an insoluble modern problem. They sat at the long table on the low platform at the front of the hall, usually reserved for the honourees at some festivity or other, or, on Saturdays for the rock band, flanking our County Council representative of the time, George. He was one of our last; quite soon we became so amalgamated with the "main" that we no longer rated our own spokesman. Bigger is better, isn't it?

Facing the Mounties and our anxious-looking Council member — how could he contrive to represent all of us fairly? — sat a couple of rows of the young people, boys and girls looking thoroughly confident of their ability to handle the unusual situation, chatting and joking with each other. Behind them on the hard chairs were the rows of complainers who had caused all the bother, the older folk who had learnt to drive aeons earlier when a vehicle was something to be used merely for getting from one place to another for some useful purpose, not for fun and games. Alone, at the very back of the hall in the shadows, sat Gus, just watching.

George, a bit uncertain and embarrassed, got to his feet, introduced the guests as best he could, and tried to explain why the meeting we had all come to had been called. It was not just the damage being done to our poor old road, the clouds of dust kicked up in dry weather by speeding wheels, the gravel flying out of the craters in it recently repaired by the grand new grader. Worse was the racket the young people made roaring up and down from one end of the Island to the other, especially late at night and, even more important, the danger they posed. Of course we all knew that nobody had been killed so far (I thought of Martin's "Hand over the Island"). But there had been some near misses lately, and quite a bit of damage to roadside fences and barns. Maybe, George wondered hopefully, it was time to take stock, and maybe the Officers sitting beside him could help us sort things out. The old people nodded, the young still grinned and nudged each other, and I was wondering if perhaps we were developing an insular variety of that new disease now ravaging Europe known as Road Rage; the waiting rooms of psychotherapists are full of its victims, we hear. The Mounties, well-trained, waited and watched.

Until quite recently we very rarely called the Law over; almost every spot of trouble we could manage ourselves, or ignore until it passed. Perhaps the last time anyone sought the help of the Oldham H.Q. was the night three or four years ago that Josh got to drinking and flew into a rage at his wife. When he brought out his gun, she fled, ran around the cove, and took refuge, sobbing, at Desmond and Marian's place. They hid her in an upstairs bedroom, and, fearing that the furious man would follow her, they telephoned Herb for help; he lived only a couple of hundred yards away, and, gentle as he is with the wood he carves, he was still the strongest man on the Island. But Herb intimated that muscles weren't much good against guns and wisely declined to come. Time to call the Mounties, thought Desmond. In due course a couple of them obligingly tied up in their boat, hitched a drive round the bay, and knocked on the door. By then the emergency was over: Josh had fired a few shots into the kitchen ceiling when his wife refused to come down and then collapsed at Marian's table exhausted. There he instantly fell asleep, his head on his arms.

Nobody had thought of summoning the police when Jem Baxter, thoroughly provoked by Jeff one summer evening, drove his old car to the sloping cliff-top, hopped out neatly, gave it a shove, and watched it smash onto the rocks below. At that time the couple had five or six young children cooped up with them in their little house stuck away on a back trail. Despite her occasional tempestuous outbursts, blowsy Jem was not a bad mother I used to think watching her patiently rowing her younger kids over the shot-silk waters of the bay on still August evenings, sharing her pleasure in it with them. Times were changing, however, as the children grew older, and the Baxters moved with the times more quickly than most of us did. When the oldest boy became a nuisance to them the parents called the mainland authorities to deal with him. Once he had received the appropriate "discipline" and "counselling" he returned home and shortly afterwards tried to take his parents to court for cruelty. Tit for tat. One morning not long ago I got talking on the ferry from Oldham to a pleasant-looking young woman I had never seen before. She soon volunteered that she represented the R.S.P.C.A. and was coming over to investigate a complaint — a Baxter daughter had said her brother was abusing her pet rabbits, setting his dog onto them. Behind the young official sat two quiet young Mounties, reading newspapers. "I asked them to come with me," whispered the girl, indicating the Mounties, "just in case of trouble. That family, you know..." A nice outing for the young men, anyhow, I thought. I never heard what happened to the rabbits, but it was plain that all the Baxters had moved more expertly into the tag end of the twentieth century than some of us had.

A Treasured Island

"Solidarity" was an old mainland word shouted once by oppressed industrial workers looking for some justice, and adopted later by other groups who had come to see themselves as equally oppressed. It implied the need for organised united action and strategic planning in the face of a specific social threat, an "enemy." On the Island it would have meant, had anyone used it, something more primitive; the random immediate answer to a sudden need was the trigger for joint action, the way we survived. At the Meeting it became plain that the young had instinctively figured out something of the modern meaning of "solidarity." They had their simple weapons ready, knew the weaknesses of their elders in this modern world, and were confident that they could remain kings of our short road.

For a long time there had been bridges between the generations; the necessary shared work had been a bond from one to the other, even if not always a welcome one to the young. There was not much time then for most people, young or old, to indulge themselves with no thought for anybody else. Neighbour and I can both smile when we hear that universities today offer courses in "Leisure Studies." "Leisure" was not a word we heard in our youth, on different continents, in different circumstances. Since we seldom had much free time we never wondered what to do with it; and like any other young creatures, in our childhood we knew how to play and amuse ourselves without bothering other people. And in our old age we still do not suffer from boredom, whatever other problems we may have. Now things were different; T.V. was the important teacher and having absorbed the lessons it brought them through the air the kids could afford to grin smugly to each other. Although they were still confined, geographically isolated, with all

The Laws of Which Land

those old folk by the water, they sensed the sudden fragility of the old ways. The power had passed across the dividing chasm: it was no longer the indigenous moral imperatives but the new savvy which counted now.

The tactful Mounties rose one by one to make suggestions on how to ensure our entire island was safe for everybody. Was it time, asked the first, to make drivers' licenses mandatory on the Island as they were in the rest of the province? Muffled guffaws from the young, frowns from the back rows. The front rows were not about to wait until they were over the hill at sixteen to begin driving and then have to obey foolish rules. The old knew that they themselves might not all manage to pass that fancy written test on the mainland, however sensibly they drove at home; and of course the young were aware of this fortunate impediment, too. So the government fiat which exempted us from that strange law stood. There was no support for the idea, obviously, although no member of the audience explained why.

The second Mountie suggested vehicle inspections might be a good thing. This also did not go down well with either group. The old people had long since figured out how to keep a truck running; possibly a few of the elders were thinking that fixing an old motor was less difficult than building a boat from scratch, with only a tiny half-model to go by. The young, of course, had quickly picked up the know-how because they wanted it for their own purposes. Why bring so-called mechanics over from the "main" to tell us what to do, and, with them, all sorts of expensive regulations? Who really needs a muffler, for instance?

The Mounties persevered, mooting one solution after another; but when they finally sailed home, duly thanked by George, only one thing had been agreed. Speed-limit signs (50 km.p.h., as in a mainland town) would be put up all along the road; and they were too, most efficiently, a month later. Naturally the young paid no attention to them — there was no lawman around to watch that they obeyed, and bother them if they didn't. The old folk, of course, had never driven that fast anyhow. If they did any joyriding, it was likely to be scarcely more rapid than the occasional summer sunset jaunt old Isaac used to take years ago round the bay on his small tractor. His wife travelled happily with him (had he contrived a special seat beside him for her?), and they progressed at about ten miles an hour, stopping altogether from time to time to chat with someone on the road. I don't think Isaac ever acquired a truck; I never saw him in one.

Fortunately the Road Rage problem solved itself without further legal input; that particular crop of youngsters grew up quite quickly, married and settled down to build their own houses and raise children, took to fishing seriously or moved to the mainland to work; the group which followed them was smaller and less boisterous. But the bug of litigiousness has now infected more of us, and it seems that the Mounties these days are getting a lot of calls concerning land feuds; we can no longer handle such difficulties ourselves, even though there are far fewer of us. Belatedly and suddenly the twentieth century has washed over us, and now the remaining Islanders must forget a brief acquaintance with it and plunge on into the dubious twenty-first. The young are likely to be more adaptable than their elders; but one may wonder what Laws they will find governing the great Net, the World Wide Web, which they will soon have to deal with.

For Island children, a net used to be something their

The Laws of Which Land

fathers regularly spread out up on the pasture land in order to check each mesh and repair it as necessary for more work in the water; and webs lay like lace handkerchiefs scattered over the grass, hung with diamond dew in the early morning sun. Those were the days when "the common round, the daily task will furnish all I need to ask" were words which could be repeated with conviction. What new proverbs and sayings are waiting for us to replace those which have survived so long?

Chapter 16

Sea Changes

Wide sea, that one continuous murmur breeds
Along the pebbled shore of memory.
— Keats

October ceased being mouse-month several years ago, thanks both to William's ingenuity and to his and Neighbour's soft hearts. One of the wild cats from the hill had chosen to give birth to a litter deep inside Leonard's wood-pile, and he was bothered, being a gentle soul, about the kittens' mewing, but reluctant to disturb them. Pat had moved out of the house long since, so Leonard was alone with the problem. Time to go up to Neighbour's for help, as he had in more urgent crises when he was trying to care for his increasingly witless mother before the Old Peoples' Home took her over.

"What you need is a cat-trap," said William, and went off to his workshop to devise one.

It worked: one by one four of the kittens were lured into it. The fifth the fierce mother dragged off by the nape of its neck to the woods, apparently. There was no more mewing; Leonard could fetch his firewood in peace.

"What are you going to do with them?" I asked William as he carried the little creatures home in his invention, something vaguely related to a lobster-trap.

"Drown 'em, I 'spose." He was gruff. Two were, in the

event, adopted by other folk and two Neighbour kept herself. The couple of cats she already had, lazy old fellows, were jealous; but the youngsters, not surprisingly given their ancestry, soon took to hunting on the land. Those brothers guarded us like ruthless tigers and no mouse entered our house again. The predators of course had the best of two worlds — exciting spying work from dawn to dusk, and a warm luxurious berth by Neighbour's stove when they felt like relaxing. It was a useful change for them and for me.

October however is still the month when one may become bewitched by an enormously swollen blood-tinged moon rising over the hill across the bay; and when one must gather in the last of the harvest for the winter's food — a few over-grown zucchinis, a row of carrots, the remaining leeks, green tomatoes unaware that summer is over — and prepare to sow the cover crop of fall rye or clover. To work, woman, I told myself and opened the west door to get down to it.

The herring-gull halted me. It was standing on the grass, immobile, profiled against the grey stones of the sunken-garden wall. Gulls, wheeling in shining clouds in the wind, circling apparently for fun on the warm-air currents rising on the headland or strung out in long streamers on the rippled bay facing the wind, wherever it is blowing from, awaiting the return of the fish-boats, are a pleasure to the eye. Waddling in groups over the land on still, foggy mornings in May and June, reduced to grubbing for worms, they are awkward and clumsy. Standing alone, silent, by the wall, this one was unnaturally large, and frightening: it should have lifted, soared out to sea as I approached slowly; but it did not. Its left eye watched me, yellow, staring, transparent: was I looking straight through its head? Nothing moved, not the air, not the great bird. I turned and walked quickly back to the house.

From the window an hour later I saw the creature lying on the grass, shining wings spread wide, neck gracefully curved. That summer two other younger, smaller gulls had died near the garden, but they had fallen victim to prowling feral cats from the woods. Gleaming feathers were scattered all around, signs of a lethal fight. They had died by cruel accident, not by that slow, almost human, process I had intruded upon. The visible ebbing of any creature's life causes the witness to listen to her own breath, count her heartbeat. Now that all that remained was cold flesh under the still shining feathers, I was able to approach it; but I was glad that its eye was veiled. A Gaelic saying told me long ago that only three things are beautiful in death: a human child, a blackcock and a sea-trout. I would have to add this great white bird.

Gulls of both sorts are as much a part of our surroundings as the rocks and the sea. The sleek black-backs mingle easily with the crowds of more plebeian herring-gulls idling on the bay in expectation of an easy meal but they seldom deign to grub for worms on the land. Recent times have been good for all gulls; and their population has grown rapidly. As their sharp eyes spy from the air what is going on below on the land and water they take stock of our new prosperity. They are affluent birds now, and like us have rising expectations of more food for less work; it is their turn to cash in on the lazy habits the modern world has allowed Islanders to develop. Instead of feeding the land, the fish-heads now feed the birds; after all, it is quicker and easier to buy a sack of fertilizer and scatter it than to save the offal and spread it, the fishermen realise. The gulls have now become importunately voracious and a real nuisance. One evening Ernest brought us a dozen fat mackerel, which M.D. began to clean by the back door. Needing a sharper knife he nipped into the kitchen to find one, and as he stepped out again one minute later was just in time to see a flock of gulls making off with every last one of the fish. Nothing left for supper or the freezer for us. Did those clever birds watch Ernest walk up the driveway with his gift, hidden in a bag, and wait, like any human thief, for the right instant to make a "hit"?

I am not alone in fearing those winged scoundrels, who will even tear their own young to pieces for food. They may be contributing these days to the decline of our population of smaller, weaker birds who lack those brutal beaks, those cunning eyes.

The other morning as I stood at the kitchen sink, washing lettuce leaves and amused by the snail climbing cautiously up the side of the dishpan, waving its eyes at me with apparent curiosity, I heard a tiny tapping sound at the window pane, turned, and saw a minute ruby-throated hummingbird sending a message through the baffling glass. Was it asking for help.? Odd behaviour, and too late in the season to be here, anyhow, for the poor little thing. I remembered the tale Ernest told us last year of how he had tried in vain to save a few infant swallows. We all used to feel our spirits rise when the swallows returned, signifying summer at last. They would perch by the score on the long telephone line to the house, even mate there. Neighbour, seeing them so busily occupied one early May morning as she walked down for a brief visit, remarked with natural admiration as she came into the house, "Amazing how clever they are at it, balanced up there on a piece of wire!" But that was several years ago.

Only occasionally does Ernest visit in our kitchen; when he does we know it will be a late bed-time for us. He always has a great deal of up-to-date information to impart, garnered from his continuous and careful observation of what is going on under the water, on the land and in the air. Just recently he called us down to his small wharf to see what was happening to his thin catch; a dozen handsome fish lay there, each with its belly torn open by seals. Bravely, he tries to enlighten the Department of Fisheries and other experts about the sinister developments he has noticed; but not many people, whether in Government or on the Island, listen to him, which is a frustration. P.R. is not, unfortunately, his forté.

Ernest is a small and skinny fellow, weather-beaten but wiry, greying hair in a fringe over his deeply furrowed forehead. He seems to be permanently worried by what he has observed and distressed by his inability to do anything much about it all. Not surprisingly, he has come to see the world in a somewhat Manichean light: fish and fowl, plant and insect, animal and human, everything is divided into Good and Evil; and there is endless war between them. When it comes to birds, pheasants and swallows fall into the Good category, sparrows and gulls into the Evil one.

Some years ago Ernest knocked at our door early one winter's evening. His face was blue with the cold and in his arms he cradled a fine bright-eyed cock pheasant.

"I was walking back home for supper," he said, "when I seen spots of fresh blood on the snow, so I followed the trail across the land halfway to the school. This bird's what I found; some fool had shot at it." Slow scarlet drops continued to fall onto the snowy doorstep from its breast. "Thought you'd likely be catching the ferry this evening, might take it to a vet. In Oldham..."We were, in fact, almost ready to leave, but scurried around, found a long basket in which to carry the wounded bird, and set off for the wharf. When we returned to the Island a couple of days later we had to report to Ernest that the handsome creature had died, peacefully, on the voyage over. It stands stuffed in the city museum now, its Island provenance duly noted in a label. The swallow story was rather different but also had a sad ending. Hoping to encourage the now rare swallows, Ernest built a few nesting boxes over one winter, nailed them up, and was gratified when a couple of the birds set up housekeeping in one of them; he watched with pleasure as they laid their eggs and hatched them. But one morning he found the four scrawny nestlings dead on the ground beneath their home; marauding sparrows had turfed the helpless creatures out and appropriated their dwelling. Ernest, in a fury, plotted his revenge on Evil carefully, waited until the sparrows' own nestlings had been hatched, and then one morning turfed them out himself — and called the cat.

"That'll teach 'em," he said, drumming with his knotty fingers on the old pine table, eyes fierce. Will it? If it did, those sparrow parents did not share their new knowledge with their fellows who usurped the pretty boxes M.D. put up. He had placed each one properly secluded from the others, since swallows, like many of us, prefer a modicum of privacy. Perhaps sparrows, like humans, are slow at learning from the mistakes of their fellows; and, of course, having no cat, we did not reinforce Ernest's striking lesson with the squatters who took over from our swallows. We miss those graceful birds on summer evenings. However, the mosquitoes are delighted by their absence. Good never triumphs, but we must hope that Evil doesn't either — not permanently, anyhow. These days Ernest appears to be increasingly overwhelmed by the dimensions of the battle, and his own health is beginning to suffer from his mounting frustration.

* * *

We were not inclined to go deeply into the teasing problems of Good and Evil with our guest at Jacob's old table, so we merely listened as he poured out his troubles; but at least we understood his language. At our last kitchen session with Ernest it occurred to me that possibly some of his difficulty when he tried to enlighten the mainland experts, apart from his lack of tact, stemmed from the fact that by now most of those people can only understand the lingo of their peers.

It used to take several decades for new words or phrases, invented to fit some grand discovery about society, the human or the rest of nature, to put down roots somewhere and spread widely. These days we are only granted a few months to try to decipher the latest fashionable expression — one which may, of course, sometimes be an old word suddenly endowed with a peculiar new meaning, or deprived of almost any. Some of us find this great Age of Communication and Public Relations confusing. At times I feel almost as old as Confucius who, advising a new emperor on how to restore order in the empire, told the man: "Return their meanings to the words."

* * *

Here on the Island the gulls go on communicating with each other in their own primitive way, as we used to do in ours; for the moment they are still confident of their supremacy around our beaches. But before long they too may have to change their plans and go elsewhere, as the great draggers from Europe did: we no longer see those hideous vessels three miles offshore scouring the sea.

One change always begets another, but now the experts are so clever that they can come up with what they perceive to be the necessary remedy for some problem they have caused with remarkable speed, dizzying speed to some of us who were born early in this century or have lived our lives in remote places, such as islands, frontier villages. From our insular point of view it looks as if the newly begotten problems multiply much faster than the efficient remedies. Was it Goethe who said: "All beginnings are delightful, the threshold is the… place to pause?" About the only place you find a pause today is in an old music score.

* * *

The sea change thrust upon M.D. and me was not due to lack of home-grown food, persecution or a desire for new horizons but merely to advancing years, 155 of them between us, and the best of those lived as Islanders. The farewell to that chapter of our lives occurred as simply and unexpectedly as our arrival twenty-four years earlier had. We crossed the water for the last time content because, providentially, a brave and remarkably suitable young couple (less than a hundred years between them) had turned up; they were willing and able to take over Jacob's acres and the old house. I fear I did not warn them that a variety of ghosts came with the property; but I suspected they would be capable of dealing with the supernatural as well as the natural, one way or another.

A Treasured Island

On our final evening the Islanders threw a party to speed us on our way. It turned out to be a pretty grand occasion; we were glad we had packed our work-clothes and tidied ourselves up before going over to the Centre. (I was touched when Amy later told me that my one city dress "looked some nice," and that now she knew I had a waist still.) We were invited to sit at the slightly raised table of honour, normally reserved for new brides or other important people, and, once, for the Mounties. Fortunately, Neighbour and William and a couple of other friends were allowed to keep us company up there, or we would have found the air too rarefied. Looking around from our exalted position I could see that even some old friends from earlier days who now lived on the "main" had come back to join the crowded celebration, including the first ferry captain we knew and his wife; one of their sons now runs the boat. The whole thing must have required a great deal of exemplary community organisation, I was thinking when the Deacon from the church up the hill, in his Sunday suit, rose to deliver what almost amounted to a premature funeral eulogy. It was as far from the truth as such things always are, but heartwarming nevertheless in its exaggeration of the few useful contributions we were said to have made to the little community. Of course we had much more to thank the Islanders for than *vice versa*. M.D. mentioned a few of them in his little speech of thanks. He recalled, for instance, the brilliant rescue by four good men of the old Jeep from the rising sea: they had spied it perched on the rocks on the beach after his absent-minded wife had failed one afternoon to put the necessary stones under its front wheels when she parked it near the house allowing it to slip silently down the hill to a watery grave. She had not even noticed it was missing from its proper berth; but it was a mercy those kind men had, and done something about it, right away. There were dozens and dozens of other kindnesses given us.

After the speeches and the splendid food served up by the women, there was lusty singing to the accompaniment of the musical Deacon's guitar; for a moment I thought we were in for a good old Revival meeting as "Amazing Grace" echoed round the hall. To wrap up the cheerful proceedings, two of the women rose to read touching poems they had written, and Betsy presented us with an elegant brass plaque on a slab of oak. It bore an etching of the Island's shoreline and the message, "We pack up our memories and continue on life's journey," and was signed, "Farewell from the people of the Island." Betsy and a lot of other people had put a great deal of work into this particular party. These sort of simple, home-made celebratory events used to be part of the cement that kept any small community going; I hoped there would be many more on the Island long after we were gone... As we left the gathering, Betsy's kind mother slipped us a memorial bottle of her home-made blueberry wine; and when we went out to the famous Jeep we found it had been decked with balloons by the children. They were floating all around it in the fading light, ready to lift us off for our last chapter.

* * *

Last night to watch the moon go up the sky "with a star or two beside," listen to the murmur of the water. "The tides and their mistress the moon." Too bad busybody men couldn't leave her alone to get on with her reliable work... Then it was the last voyage out in the morning.

Over the years it had become a habit to employ that

A Treasured Island

hiatus at sea, coming or going, to concoct mental lists of "things to be done at once." This time I just tried to make one of "things learnt on the Island." It turned out to be odd, and included a number of interesting lessons which might not be very useful in the future in the city.

It began thus:

1. Ancient paint on woodwork which, they say, was made from ox-blood and milk, can only be removed by ammonia; it resists everything else.
2. Dried sea-weed is quite an effective insulation in walls.
3. Abandoned ant-hills provide plenty of beautifully sieved soil for the use of tree- and bush-planters.
4. Grapevines thrive on suffering. (That was heard first in Italy, proved true here.)
5. Carrots make a pretty, pale wine.
6. Pablum baby food may be lethal to infant bats. (Betsy adopted an orphaned bat once, she carried it everywhere with her and it thrived on the milk she fed it through an eye-dropper. When, on the advice of a mainland vet, she added Pablum to its diet, the little creature promptly died.)

But if most of this odd knowledge picked up over the years should now be relegated to my cluttered mental lumber-room, one or two of our offspring were still probably using snippets of Island lore gathered on visits. The Yukoner, for instance, found out something about how to build this and that, and especially staircases; a rumour reached us that he is famous for constructing such things in his corner of the globe. Perhaps he also figured out a thing or two about how to captain a team when he enlisted a bunch of his buddies from Gus's Saturday night gatherings to help him build a very high rock sea-wall to defeat the waves about to undermine the cliff on which we grow our food. William, down to survey the operation from up above the workers, turned to me and said: "That boy'll make a good foreman one day." Memorable music to the ears of a parent about to shoot the last arrow into the wild blue yonder. And the artistic daughter, the musician son, probably picked up some inspiration from our surroundings when they visited. The latter never noticed Jacob on the prowl in the house, but he did see a strange woman in black looking out of the attic window. Samuel's widow?

The ferry docked with a bump against the Oldham wharf and that was the end of stashing away inconsequential lessons in an inefficient human brain. It was time to learn to deal with the rational memory in M.D.'s computers, enter the current New Age. There must have been a dozen of them since I was born, when Annie Besant and a variety of other contradictory prophets were all the rage. It should be possible to survive one more, briefly anyhow.

We took the long road following the shore to the city; and that evening we caught a glimpse of the faithful moon above the house-tops before a flurry of clouds obscured her.